FINANCIAL INSTITUTIONS AND SERVICES

# THE CONSUMER FINANCIAL PROTECTION BUREAU

## OVERVIEW AND ANALYSES

# FINANCIAL INSTITUTIONS AND SERVICES

Additional books in this series can be found on Nova's website under the Series tab.

Additional e-books in this series can be found on Nova's website under the e-books tab.

# ECONOMIC ISSUES, PROBLEMS AND PERSPECTIVES

Additional books in this series can be found on Nova's website under the Series tab.

Additional e-books in this series can be found on Nova's website under the e-books tab.

FINANCIAL INSTITUTIONS AND SERVICES

# THE CONSUMER FINANCIAL PROTECTION BUREAU

## OVERVIEW AND ANALYSES


PAUL J. CERUTTI
AND
MARGARET KOLCHAK
EDITORS



nova publishers
*New York*

For permission to use material from this book please contact us:
Telephone 631-231-7269; Fax 631-231-8175
Web Site: http://www.novapublishers.com



Additional color graphics may be available in the e-book version of this book.

**Library of Congress Cataloging-in-Publication Data**

ISBN 978-1-62257-637-1

*Published by Nova Science Publishers, Inc. † New York*

# CONTENTS

# PREFACE

In the wake of the worst U.S. financial crisis since the Great Depression, Congress passed and the President signed into law sweeping reforms of the financial services regulatory system through the Dodd-Frank Wall Street Reform and Consumer Protection Act. This book provides an overview of the regulatory structure of consumer finance under existing federal law before the Dodd-Frank Act went into effect and examines arguments for modifying the regime in order to more effectively regulate consumer financial markets. Also analyzed is how the CFP Act changes the legal structure, with a focus on the Bureau's organization; the entities and activities that fall and do not fall under the Bureau's supervisory, enforcement, and rulemaking authorities; the Bureau's general and specific rulemaking powers and procedures; and the Bureau's findings.

Chapter 1 - In the wake of the worst U.S. financial crisis since the Great Depression, Congress passed and the President signed into law sweeping reforms of the financial services regulatory system through the Dodd-Frank Wall Street Reform and Consumer Protection Act (Dodd-Frank Act), P.L. 111- 203. Title X of the Dodd-Frank Act is entitled the Consumer Financial Protection Act of 2010 (CFP Act). The CFP Act establishes the Bureau of Consumer Financial Protection (CFPB or Bureau) within the Federal Reserve System (FRS) with rulemaking, enforcement, and supervisory powers over many consumer financial products and services, as well as the entities that sell them. The CFP Act significantly enhances federal consumer protection regulatory authority over nondepository financial institutions, potentially subjecting them to analogous supervisory, examination, and enforcement standards that have been applicable to depository institutions in the past. The act also transfers to the Bureau much of the consumer compliance authority over larger depositories that previously had been held by banking regulators.

Additionally, the Bureau acquired the authority to write rules to implement most federal consumer financial protection laws that previously was held by a number of other federal agencies. Although the powers that the CFPB has at its disposal are largely the same or analogous to those that other federal regulators have held for decades, there is a great deal of uncertainty in how the new agency will exercise these broad and flexible authorities, especially in light of its almost exclusive focus on consumer protection. As a result, the CFP Act has proven to be one of the more controversial portions of the financial reform legislation. The 112$^{th}$ Congress is actively involved in conducting oversight of the implementation of the CFP Act. Additionally, the 112$^{th}$ Congress has considered a number of bills that would significantly alter the structure of the Bureau. For example, H.R. 2434, the Financial Services and General Government Appropriations Act, 2012, would make the CFPB's primary funding subject to the traditional appropriations process, and H.R. 1315, the Consumer Financial Protection Safety and Soundness Improvement Act, would convert the CFPB's leadership structure from a sole directorship to a commission and would allow the newly established Financial Stability Oversight Council (FSOC) to overturn CFPB-issued regulations with a simple majority vote, as opposed to the current super majority requirement. H.R. 2434 was reported favorably out of the House Committee on Appropriations, and H.R. 1315 was referred to the Senate Committee on Banking, Housing, and Urban Affairs after passing the full House by a vote of 241 to 173. Additionally, 44 Senators signed a letter to the President expressing support for the Bureau-related objectives of H.R. 2434 and H.R. 1315. This report provides an overview of the regulatory structure of consumer finance under existing federal law before the Dodd-Frank Act went into effect and examines arguments for modifying the regime in order to more effectively regulate consumer financial markets. It then analyzes how the CFP Act changes that legal structure, with a focus on the Bureau's organization; the entities and activities that fall (and do not fall) under the Bureau's supervisory, enforcement, and rulemaking authorities; the Bureau's general and specific rulemaking powers and procedures; and the Bureau's funding.

Chapter 2 - High default and foreclosure rates in the housing market have resulted in questions as to whether borrowers were fully informed about the terms of their mortgage loans. A lack of transparency with respect to loan terms and settlement costs can make it difficult for consumers to make well-informed decisions when choosing mortgage products. In addition, inadequate disclosures can make some borrowers more vulnerable to predatory lending or discriminatory practices. The adequate disclosure of mortgage terms is a longstanding issue that has prompted several congressional actions. For example, the Truth in Lending Act (TILA) of 1968 and the Real Estate Settlement Procedures Act (RESPA) of 1974 were enacted to require disclosures of credit costs and terms to borrowers. The Economic Growth and Regulatory Paperwork Reduction Act of 1996 (P.L. 104-208) directed the Federal Reserve Board and the Department of Housing and Urban Development (HUD) to propose a single form that satisfied the requirements of RESPA and TILA. However, the Federal Reserve Board and HUD concluded that regulatory changes would not be sufficient and that further statutory changes would be required for the forms to be consolidated. More recently, the Dodd-Frank Wall Street Reform and Consumer Protection Act of 2010 (Dodd-Frank Act; P.L. 111-203), which established the Consumer Financial Protection Bureau (CFPB), mandated the new agency revisit disclosure stipulations for mortgage loans. In addition, the Dodd-Frank Act requires the CFPB to consolidate mandatory TILA and RESPA disclosures into one Loan Estimate form. The 112$^{th}$ Congress has been closely monitoring the subsequent rulemaking associated with the Dodd-Frank Act, as well as the performance and effectiveness of the CFPB. Consequently, this report examines one of the first major actions undertaken by the new agency. Specifically, efforts by the CFPB to create an effective mortgage disclosure form for borrowers are discussed.

Chapter 3 - The Consumer Financial Protection Bureau (CFPB) was established by Title X of the Dodd-Frank Wall Street Reform and Consumer Financial Protection Act (P.L. 111-203, the Dodd-Frank Act). The creation of the CFPB consolidates many existing consumer financial protection responsibilities into one agency. The Dodd-Frank Act states that the purpose of the CFPB is to implement and enforce federal consumer financial law while ensuring that consumers can access financial products and services. The CFPB is also instructed to ensure that the markets for consumer financial services and products are fair, transparent, and competitive. To fulfill its mandate, the CFPB can issue rules, examine certain institutions, and enforce consumer protection laws and regulations. On January 4, 2012, President Obama installed Richard Cordray as the director of the Consumer Financial Protection Bureau via recess appointment. The CFPB could not exercise its new powers until a director was appointed. Included in the newly established powers is the authority to regulate certain nonbanks for consumer protection. Under the new authority conferred by the appointment of Cordray, the CFPB announced the Nonbank Supervision Program. A nonbank is an institution that provides financial services but does not have a bank, thrift, or credit union charter. The

Nonbank Supervision Program will subject some nonbanks to the same consumer protection standards as currently applied to banks. Under the program, the CFPB will supervise three groups of nonbanks. First, the CFPB can regulate nonbanks in three specific markets— mortgage companies, payday lenders, and private education lenders. Second, the CFPB can regulate the "larger participants" in other financial markets. Third, the CFPB may supervise a nonbank that is performing actions that may pose a risk to consumers with regard to consumer financial products or services. This report describes the Nonbank Supervision Program as well as other initiatives that the CFPB has started since its creation. This report does not address arguments that have been made against the validity of the recess appointment itself, nor does it address related questions that have been raised regarding the scope of Cordray's authority as the director of the CFPB while serving pursuant to a recess appointment.

Chapter 4 - Title X of the Dodd-Frank Wall Street Reform and Consumer Protection Act (P.L. 111-203, July 21, 2010) consolidates many federal consumer protection responsibilities into a new Bureau of Consumer Financial Protection (often referred to as the Consumer Financial Protection Bureau, or CFPB) within the Federal Reserve System. The act transfers supervisory and enforcement authority over a number of consumer financial products and services to the Bureau on a still-to-be-determined transfer date during calendar year 2011. Title X and Title XIV of the act contain numerous provisions that require or permit the CFPB to issue regulations implementing the statute's provisions. This report describes those provisions, notes that certain regulatory oversight tools will not be available for CFPB rules, and discusses the authority of a council of bank regulators to "set aside" the Bureau's rules. Section 1022 alone gives the CFPB broad rulemaking powers, authorizing it to prescribe such rules "as may be necessary or appropriate" to enable the Bureau to administer federal consumer financial protection laws. The act contains many other provisions that require or permit the Bureau to issue rules, most of which give the Bureau substantial discretion regarding whether rules need to be issued, the contents of those rules, and when they must be issued. The Bureau also assumes responsibility for certain transferor agencies' existing rules, proposed rules that have not been made final, and final rules that have not taken effect. Therefore, other than for about 20 rules that are specifically required in the statute, it is not currently possible to determine how many rules the Bureau will issue, or the contents of those rules. Although most of the Bureau's rulemaking authority and discretion is the same as it was before being transferred from the safety and soundness (prudential) regulators, it is not clear that those authorities and discretion will be exercised in the same way. Like other independent regulatory agencies, some regulatory oversight methods will not be available for CFPB rules. The Bureau's significant rules will not be reviewed by the Office of Management and Budget (OMB) under Executive Order 12866, and those rules will not be subject to the cost-benefit analysis requirements in the order. The Bureau may be able to void OMB disapprovals of its collections of information under the Paperwork Reduction Act. Because the CFPB might not receive appropriated funds, Congress may not be able to control the Bureau's rulemaking through appropriations restrictions. Also, the effectiveness of new requirements placed on the Bureau to examine its rules within five years, and to take certain actions under the Regulatory Flexibility Act, may depend on how the Bureau interprets key terms. Congress did, however, empower the newly created Financial Stability Oversight Council (composed primarily of the heads of the prudential regulatory agencies from which the CFPB was formed) to "stay" or "set aside" all or part of a Bureau rule that it concludes would put the safety and soundness of the U.S. banking or financial systems at risk. No other executive branch entity (including OMB) has previously been given the authority to nullify an agency's rules, and the authority to set aside a portion of a rule is greater than the expedited authority Congress gave itself through the Congressional Review Act (CRA). However, several aspects of the Council review process are currently unclear (e.g., whether the Council must vote to stay a rule). Although Congress may not be able to use appropriations restrictions to control CFPB rulemaking, Congress still has an array of oversight tools available, including confirmation hearings, oversight hearings, meetings between individual Members and the Bureau, and CRA resolutions of disapproval.

Chapter 5 - The Consumer Financial Protection Bureau (CFPB) was launched on July 21, 2011 with a focused goal: To make the markets for consumer financial products work for consumers, responsible providers, and the economy as a whole. They wanted to make sure that the price and risks of financial products are clear so that consumers can decide what products are best for them. And they wanted to make sure that there are sensible rules of the road and a level playing field so that providers can innovate and compete fairly. The CFPB was created on July 21, 2010 by the Dodd-Frank Wall Street Reform and Consumer Protection Act. Before the Dodd-Frank Act, responsibility for administering and enforcing the various federal consumer financial laws was scattered across seven different federal agencies. For each of those seven agencies, consumer protection was only one of its responsibilities. The result was that no single agency was truly on the hook for protecting the average, everyday user of financial products and services. There was no true accountability, and consumers got left behind. The Dodd-Frank Act changed this by creating in the CFPB a single point of accountability for consumer financial protection. And they were given, for the first time at the Federal level, supervisory authority over independent nonbank companies in addition to depositories. That means, for example, that when it comes to the mortgage market, they will be able to ensure that brokers, originators, and servicers play by the same rules regardless of their charter. It doesn't matter if you're a thrift, bank, finance company, ILC, or investment bank. If you want to be in the business of consumer finance, then you've got to play by the same rules as everybody else. They recognize that the CFPB has a tough job. But fortunately, they have lots of tools in our toolkit – research, supervision, rulemaking, enforcement, and consumer education. Having the full range of tools means that they don't have to force a square policy peg into a round hole. They will strive to use each of these tools in the smartest way possible, matching problems to solutions. Ultimately, our efforts will benefit the entire economy. They will help give families the confidence they need to borrow for a home or a child's education. They will help give our nation's financial institutions the confidence they need to innovate and compete. If they succeed in our mission, everybody wins. As required by the Dodd-Frank Act, the CFPB prepared financial statements for fiscal year 2011. The Government Accountability Office (GAO) rendered an unqualified -- or "clean" -- audit opinion on the CFPB's financial statements. GAO noted no material weaknesses or significant deficiencies in CFPB's internal controls and cited no instances of noncompliance with laws and regulations. The CFPB's first Financial Report describes the fiscal year 2011 efforts to establish the CFPB, and the results they have achieved to date.

Chapter 6 - The Consumer Financial Protection Bureau ("CFPB" or "Bureau") began consumer response operations on July 21, 2011 and became the first federal agency solely focused on consumer financial protection. The Dodd-Frank Wall Street Reform and Consumer Protection Act of 2010 ("Dodd-Frank Act") created the Bureau to protect consumers of financial products or services and to encourage the fair and competitive operation of consumer financial markets. Taking in, resolving, and analyzing consumer complaints[1] is an integral part of the CFPB's work, as Congress set forth in the Dodd-Frank Act.[2] The Bureau's Consumer Response team hears directly from consumers about the challenges they face in the marketplace, brings their concerns to the attention of financial institutions, and assists in addressing their complaints. The Consumer Response team began taking consumer complaints about credit cards on July 21, 2011; it began handling mortgage complaints on December 1, 2011; and it began accepting complaints about bank products and services, private student loans, and other consumer loans on March 1, 2012. The CFPB's phased-in approach to taking complaints has allowed Consumer Response to develop strong foundations over time. Based on feedback from consumers and companies, as well as its own observations, the Consumer Response team identifies new opportunities to improve its processes and implement changes with each product launch. By applying the lessons learned through previous complaint function rollouts, the Consumer Response team has improved its intake process, enhanced communication with companies, and ensured the system's ease-of-use and effectiveness for consumers. The CFPB aims to provide services that are trusted by consumers and companies alike and, by the end of 2012, expects to handle consumer complaints on all products and services under its authority. Consumers may contact the CFPB about products and services beyond those listed above. The Bureau answers these inquiries and refers consumers to other regulators or additional resources where appropriate. The CFPB also created a "Tell Your Story" feature on its website that gives consumers the opportunity to share their experiences – positive or negative – with consumer financial products and services. These submissions, like formal complaints, are reviewed by CFPB staff to help the Bureau understand current issues in the financial marketplace. In keeping with the CFPB's statutory responsibility and its commitment to accountability, this report provides an overview of how Consumer Response handles complaints and presents an analysis of complaints received over the period from July 21 through December 31, 2011.

In: The Consumer Financial Protection Bureau ISBN 978-1-62257-637-1
Editors: P. J. Cerutti and M. Kolchak 

*Chapter 1*

# THE CONSUMER FINANCIAL PROTECTION BUREAU (CFPB): A LEGAL ANALYSIS*

*David H. Carpenter*

## SUMMARY

In the wake of the worst U.S. financial crisis since the Great Depression, Congress passed and the President signed into law sweeping reforms of the financial services regulatory system through the Dodd-Frank Wall Street Reform and Consumer Protection Act (Dodd-Frank Act), P.L. 111- 203.

Title X of the Dodd-Frank Act is entitled the Consumer Financial Protection Act of 2010 (CFP Act). The CFP Act establishes the Bureau of Consumer Financial Protection (CFPB or Bureau) within the Federal Reserve System (FRS) with rulemaking, enforcement, and supervisory powers over many consumer financial products and services, as well as the entities that sell them. The CFP Act significantly enhances federal consumer protection regulatory authority over nondepository financial institutions, potentially subjecting them to analogous supervisory, examination, and enforcement standards that have been applicable to depository institutions in the past. The act also transfers to the Bureau much of the consumer compliance authority over larger depositories that previously had been held by banking regulators. Additionally, the Bureau acquired the authority to write rules to implement most federal consumer

* This is an edited, reformatted and augmented version of Congressional Research Service, Publication No. R42572, dated June 7, 2012.

financial protection laws that previously was held by a number of other federal agencies.

Although the powers that the CFPB has at its disposal are largely the same or analogous to those that other federal regulators have held for decades, there is a great deal of uncertainty in how the new agency will exercise these broad and flexible authorities, especially in light of its almost exclusive focus on consumer protection. As a result, the CFP Act has proven to be one of the more controversial portions of the financial reform legislation.

The 112$^{th}$ Congress is actively involved in conducting oversight of the implementation of the CFP Act. Additionally, the 112$^{th}$ Congress has considered a number of bills that would significantly alter the structure of the Bureau. For example, H.R. 2434, the Financial Services and General Government Appropriations Act, 2012, would make the CFPB's primary funding subject to the traditional appropriations process, and H.R. 1315, the Consumer Financial Protection Safety and Soundness Improvement Act, would convert the CFPB's leadership structure from a sole directorship to a commission and would allow the newly established Financial Stability Oversight Council (FSOC) to overturn CFPB-issued regulations with a simple majority vote, as opposed to the current super majority requirement. H.R. 2434 was reported favorably out of the House Committee on Appropriations, and H.R. 1315 was referred to the Senate Committee on Banking, Housing, and Urban Affairs after passing the full House by a vote of 241 to 173. Additionally, 44 Senators signed a letter to the President expressing support for the Bureau-related objectives of H.R. 2434 and H.R. 1315.

This report provides an overview of the regulatory structure of consumer finance under existing federal law before the Dodd-Frank Act went into effect and examines arguments for modifying the regime in order to more effectively regulate consumer financial markets. It then analyzes how the CFP Act changes that legal structure, with a focus on the Bureau's organization; the entities and activities that fall (and do not fall) under the Bureau's supervisory, enforcement, and rulemaking authorities; the Bureau's general and specific rulemaking powers and procedures; and the Bureau's funding.

## Introduction

In the wake of the worst U.S. financial crisis since the Great Depression, Congress passed and the President signed into law sweeping reforms of the financial services regulatory system through the Dodd-Frank Wall Street Reform and Consumer Protection Act (Dodd-Frank Act), P.L. 111- 203.

Title X of the Dodd-Frank Act is entitled the Consumer Financial Protection Act of 2010 (CFP Act). The CFP Act establishes the Bureau of Consumer Financial Protection (CFPB or Bureau) within the Federal Reserve System (FRS) with rulemaking, enforcement, and supervisory powers over many consumer financial products and services, as well as the entities that sell them.

The law also transfers to the Bureau the primary rulemaking authority over many federal consumer protection laws that, with one exception,[1] were enacted prior to the Dodd-Frank Act. These "enumerated consumer laws"[2] include the Truth in Lending Act[3] and the Real Estate Settlement Procedures Act.[4]

The CFP Act has proven to be one of the more controversial portions of the financial reform legislation. The 112th Congress is actively involved in conducting oversight of the implementation of the CFP Act.[5]

Additionally, the 112th Congress has considered a number of bills that would significantly alter the structure of the Bureau. For example, H.R. 2434, the Financial Services and General Government Appropriations Act, 2012, would make the CFPB's primary funding subject to the traditional appropriations process, and H.R. 1315, the Consumer Financial Protection Safety and Soundness Improvement Act, would convert the CFPB's leadership structure from a sole directorship to a commission and would allow the newly established Financial Stability Oversight Council (FSOC) to overturn CFPB-issued regulations with a simple majority vote, as opposed to the current super majority requirement.

H.R. 2434 was reported favorably out of the House Committee on Appropriations, and H.R. 1315 was referred to the Senate Committee on Banking, Housing, and Urban Affairs after passing the full House by a vote of 241 to 173. Additionally, 44 Senators signed a letter to the President expressing support for the Bureau-related objectives of H.R. 2434 and H.R. 1315.[6]

This report provides an overview of the regulatory structure of consumer finance under existing federal law before the Dodd-Frank Act went into effect and examines arguments for modifying the regime in order to more effectively regulate consumer financial markets. It then analyzes how the CFP Act changes that legal structure, with a focus on the Bureau's organization; the entities and activities that fall (and do not fall) under the Bureau's supervisory, enforcement, and rulemaking authorities; the Bureau's general and specific rulemaking powers and procedures; and the Bureau's funding.

# Federal Consumer Financial Protection Regulation Before the CFPB

Before the CFP Act went into effect, which largely occurred on July 21, 2011 (called the "designated transfer date"),[7] the authority to write rules to implement the majority of the federal consumer financial protection laws, the power to enforce these laws, and the supervisory authority over the individuals and companies offering and selling consumer financial products and services were predominately shared by five different banking regulators, as well as the Federal Trade Commission (FTC) and the Department of Housing and Urban Development (HUD). The jurisdiction of these regulators varied based on the type of institution involved and, in some cases, based on the type of financial activities in which institutions engaged.

The authority of the five banking regulators varied based on depository charters. The Office of the Comptroller of the Currency (OCC) supervised national banks; the Board of Governors of the Federal Reserve System (FRB) supervised domestic operations of foreign banks and state-chartered banks that were members of the FRS; the Federal Deposit Insurance Corporation (FDIC) supervised state-chartered banks and other state-chartered banking institutions that were not members of the FRS;[8] the National Credit Union Administration (NCUA) supervised federally insured credit unions; and the Office of Thrift Supervision (OTS)[9] supervised federal savings and loan associations and thrifts. The five banking regulators were charged with the two-pronged mandate of regulating for both safety and soundness, as well as consumer compliance. Safety and soundness regulation, also referred to as prudential regulation, consists of ensuring that institutions are managed in a safe and sound manner so as to maintain profitability and avoid failure.[10] The focus of consumer compliance regulation, on the other hand, is ensuring that institutions are in compliance with applicable consumer protection and fair lending laws.[11]

To reach these ends, the banking regulators were provided with broad authority to subject banks, credit unions, and thrifts (which this report will collectively refer to as "depository institutions" or "depositories") to up-front regulatory standards, such as maintaining minimum capital levels, through regulations, orders, and guidelines. These regulators also were given strong supervisory powers, including the authority to perform on-site examinations of depositories,[12] and flexible enforcement powers to rectify problems found during the course of their supervision.[13] These supervisory powers gave banking regulators at least the potential to catch problems before they caused significant harm to consumers, counterparties, and the depositories themselves.

Additionally, consumer compliance issues often were dealt with informally and confidentially as part of the examination process, rather than through public, *ex post* formal enforcement orders.[14]

The Federal Trade Commission (FTC) was the primary federal regulator for nondepository financial institutions, such as payday lenders and mortgage brokers.[15] Unlike the federal banking regulators, the FTC had little up-front supervisory or enforcement authority. The FTC's powers generally were limited to *ex post* enforcement. Thus, the FTC did not have the statutory authority to regularly examine nondepository financial institutions or impose reporting requirements on them as a way to proactively ensure they were complying with consumer protection laws. The FTC also did not have any direct safety and soundness authority over institutions.[16] Instead, nondepository financial institutions were primarily supervised by state regulators. The powers granted to state regulators and the level of supervision these regulators provided varied considerably from state to state.

In addition to institution-based distinctions, both depository and nondepository financial institutions also were subject to the restrictions of federal consumer financial protection laws. These federal laws each regulate specific types of consumer products and activities. For example, the Truth in Lending Act (TILA)[17] requires disclosures regarding the terms and conditions associated with extensions of consumer credit; the Equal Credit Opportunity Act (ECOA)[18] bans certain kinds of discrimination in consumer lending; the Real Estate Settlement Procedures Act of 1974 (RESPA)[19] imposes disclosure requirements and fee restrictions associated with home loan settlements; the Truth in Savings Act (TISA)[20] requires disclosures regarding the terms and conditions of consumer deposit accounts; and the Fair Debt Collection Practices Act (FDCPA)[21] restricts third-party debt collection activities.[22]

Individually, these enumerated consumer laws target discrete activities. Taken as a whole, they govern a broad and diverse set of consumer activities and services.[23] Before the Dodd-Frank Act went into effect, the rulemaking authority to implement federal consumer financial protection laws was largely held by the FRB.[24] The authority to enforce the federal consumer financial protection laws and regulations, however, was spread among all of the banking regulators, the FTC, and HUD.[25]

In short, the banking regulators held both prudential and consumer compliance supervisory and enforcement powers over depository institutions.

Although they had the authority to take *ex post* enforcement actions, the banking regulators placed a great deal of emphasis on *ex ante* regulation and supervision. The FTC was the primary regulator of nondepository financial institutions. The FTC's authority was much more limited than that of the banking regulators. Its authority was almost exclusively limited to *ex post* enforcement.[26] Additionally, both depositories and nondepository financial institutions were required to comply with the various federal consumer financial laws and the regulations issued under those laws. The rulemaking authority under the federal consumer financial laws was predominately held by the FRB, but the authority to enforce those laws and regulations was spread among all the banking regulators, as well as the FTC and HUD.[27]

## Arguments for Consolidating Federal Consumer Financial Regulatory Powers

Scholars and consumer advocates argued that the complex, fragmented federal consumer financial protection regulatory system in place before the Dodd-Frank Act failed to adequately protect consumers and created market inefficiencies to the detriment of both financial institutions and consumers. Some argued that these problems could be corrected if all federal consumer financial regulatory powers were consolidated in a single regulator with a consumer focus.[28] As discussed below, proponents of change generally raised two primary criticisms of the pre-DoddFrank Act regulatory system. One was that it allowed financial institutions to engage in "regulatory arbitrage," which pressured regulators to lower supervisory standards in a so-called "race-to-the-bottom."[29] The other was that banking regulators tended to place greater emphasis on their safety and soundness duties than their consumer compliance responsibilities.[30]

### *"Regulatory Arbitrage" Resulted in a "Race-to-the-Bottom"*

"Regulatory arbitrage," that is, a financial institution's ability to take advantage of regulatory loopholes or permissive supervisory oversight, arguably resulted from three forms of competition—competition between depositories and nondepositories; competition between the various types of depository charters (e.g., state charter versus federal charter; bank charter versus thrift charter); and competition between the financial regulators.[31] These competitive pressures were fueled by the fact that there is considerable overlap in the types of consumer products and services that are offered by state and federal depositories, as well as by nondepository institutions. However, as described in detail above, these institutions had different federal regulators and could be subject to very different regulatory regimes.[32]

Some believed that the more costly supervisory burdens of depositories gave nondepositories a competitive advantage over depository institutions in certain consumer markets.[33] The general discrepancy may have encouraged banking regulators to lower their supervisory standards as a way to help depositories under their jurisdictions more effectively compete with nondepositories.[34]

Banking regulators may have been further pressured to relax regulatory scrutiny because of the threat that depositories would change their charters. Although there were significant distinctions between the various depository charters historically, statutory changes over the years have eliminated many of those differences.[35] As a result, many depositories could change their charters without having to significantly alter their business practices.[36] One of the few remaining differences was that the depository charters determined an institution's primary regulator. Thus, an influencing factor in an institution's chartering decision could be the characteristics of the regulator associated with a particular charter. Financial institutions may be incentivized to switch their charters in order to be supervised by the agency with the lightest, least costly regulatory touch.[37]

Banking regulators also had a financial incentive to attract institutions to their charters and to ensure the happiness of institutions already within their supervisory jurisdictions because a significant portion of their budgets derive from assessments against the institutions under their supervision. [38] As a result, if one banking regulator lowered its regulatory standards as a way to encourage financial institutions to change their charters, the others may have been pressured to respond in kind.[39]

Some argued that these competitive forces placed downward pressure on regulators, which led to a "race-to-the-bottom."[40] Therefore, some proposed consolidating consumer compliance regulatory authority in a single agency as a means to level the regulatory playing field for depositories and nondepository financial institutions, thus preventing the "race-to-the-bottom" and "regulatory arbitrage" to the benefit of both consumers and financial institutions.[41]

***Safety and Soundness Historically Have Trumped Consumer Compliance***

The second major criticism of the federal consumer financial protection regulatory system before the Dodd-Frank Act was that no federal agency had both the mission and legal authority to effectively regulate consumer markets.[42]

The banking regulators had the statutory powers to protect consumers; however, it has been argued that the banking regulators placed more importance on their safety and soundness mission than on their consumer protection duties. Scholars have noted that the banking regulators view their primary mission as protecting the safety and soundness of banks, not protecting consumers.[43]

This heightened focus on safety and soundness arguably caused regulators to turn a blind eye toward practices that may have been detrimental to consumers if those practices were profitable for banks.

This safety and soundness-centric mission also may have hampered the banking regulators' ability to hire and retain staff with expertise in consumer products and consumer behavior.[44]

The FTC, on the other hand, did have a consumer focus. However, the FTC's statutory authority prevented it from conducting *ex ante* supervision of nondepositories and from regulating depositories altogether.[45]

Some argued that these statutory limitations precluded the FTC from sufficiently protecting consumers and eliminating consumer financial market inefficiencies.[46]

Professors Warren and Bar-Gill summed up these arguments this way:

> Effective regulation requires both authority and motivation. Yet none of the many regulators in the consumer credit field satisfies these basic requirements. Federal banking regulators have the authority but not the motivation. For each federal banking agency, consumer protection is not first (or even second) on its priority list. By contrast, the FTC makes consumer protection a priority, but it enjoys only limited authority over consumer credit markets.[47]

Thus, it was argued that consumer markets could be effectively regulated if a federal agency was established with both a consumer protection focus and strong supervisory, enforcement, and rulemaking powers.

## OVERVIEW OF THE BUREAU

The CFP Act significantly alters the consumer financial protection landscape by consolidating rulemaking authority and, to a lesser extent, supervisory and enforcement authority in one regulator—the CFPB. The CFP Act empowers the Bureau through the transfer of existing consumer protection powers from other federal regulators and the establishment of heightened consumer protection authorities not previously held by federal regulators. The Bureau has jurisdiction over an array of consumer financial products and services, and it serves as the primary federal consumer financial supervisor of many of the institutions that offer these products and services. However, at least six other agencies—the OCC, FRB, FDIC, NCUA, FTC, and HUD—will continue to hold some consumer protection powers.

The CFP Act also imposes certain limitations on the Bureau's authority to regulate various types of financial institutions and financial activities. Several fundamental policy questions arose consistently during the legislative debate over proposals that ultimately became the CFP Act. These policy questions seem to be the primary motivations for the exceptions to the consolidation of consumer protection power in the CFPB and the various restrictions on the Bureau's authorities.

One policy question was how best to balance the safety and soundness regulation of depositories with that of consumer compliance. There is considerable overlap between prudential and consumer compliance regulation.[48] For instance, a mortgage that the borrower is unable to fully repay is typically bad for both the borrower and the lender. The borrower runs the risk of damage to her credit score and the loss of her home. The lender may suffer from lost interest income and increased costs associated with the foreclosure process. However, there are some areas in which there can be a conflict between safety and soundness regulation and consumer protection. When a banking activity is profitable, safety and soundness regulators tend to look upon it favorably because it enables the bank to meet capital requirements and withstand financial shocks. A consumer protection regulator, on the other hand, may look at such activity less favorably if the profit is seen to have been gained unfairly or deceptively at the expense of consumers.[49]

A related question that surfaced frequently during the legislative debate is the extent to which large and small financial institutions should be treated differently in the regulatory structure.[50] Whereas the largest depository institutions are accustomed to having examiners on-site continuously, examinations may be more disruptive for smaller depositories.[51] Enhanced compliance costs also are likely to more significantly impact smaller depositories, with their lower aggregate revenues, than larger depositories. Similar arguments could be made for large versus small nondepository financial institutions. Additionally, when assessing the causes of the recent financial crisis, many tend to place more blame on this country's large financial institutions than on smaller ones.[52] Thus, one could argue that the larger institutions should be subject to greater, more costly regulation than smaller institutions. On the other hand, the goal of the Dodd-Frank Act appears to be geared not just toward eliminating the exact causes of the recent financial crisis, but also toward preventing future crises.

Another issue that the legislative drafters of the CFP Act had to grapple with is that there is not always a clear delineation between financial and nonfinancial goods, services, and providers in the marketplace. For example, a clothing store's main line of business likely is selling clothes and shoes, so it may seem that a consumer financial regulator would have no regulatory role over it. However, most clothing retailers do rely on financial services to maintain their businesses. They usually accept credit cards and debit cards as a form of payment. Many clothing stores team with financial institutions to offer credit cards that provide store rewards for using the card. Clothing retailers also commonly offer electronic gift cards. Additionally, some clothing stores may directly offer financing options for the purchase of their merchandise. As a result, defining the scope of the Bureau's authority required careful consideration. In some instances, the act uses rigid, bright-line rules that provide considerable certainty as to where the Bureau's authorities begin and end. In other instances, the CFP Act imposes subjective standards intended to give the CFPB the flexibility to evolve with consumer financial markets, but that also create the potential that the Bureau will overreach by regulating beyond congressional intent.

Apparently as a result of the policy considerations outlined above, the act's allocation of regulatory authority among the prudential regulators and the CFPB varies based on institution size and type. Regulatory authority differs for (1) depository institutions with more than $10 billion in assets (i.e., "larger depositories"); (2) depository institutions with $10 billion or less in assets (i.e., "smaller depositories"); and (3) nondepositories. The Dodd-Frank Act also explicitly exempts a number of different entities and consumer financial activities from the CFPB's supervisory, enforcement, and rulemaking authorities.

Consequently, compliance costs and the extent to which the cost and availability of credit will be affected by the new regulator will depend on the type of institution that is providing consumer financial products and services, as well as exactly how the Bureau wields its powers and how aggressively it (and other state and federal regulators) enforces consumer protection laws and regulations.

The breadth of the CFPB's supervisory, enforcement, and rulemaking powers is similar to that of the banking regulators. The banking regulators, however, have held those authorities for decades, which has established a certain level of certainty in the industry as to how those powers will be exercised. The fact that the CFPB does not have the same rich history coupled with the Bureau's overarching focus on consumers, as opposed to safety and soundness, has some anxious that the Bureau will overreach in utilizing its broad and flexible powers, which could lead to an excessive restriction in consumer credit and an undue increase in regulatory costs.[53]

## BUREAU'S PURPOSE AND STRUCTURE

The stated goal of the Bureau is to

> implement and, where applicable, enforce Federal consumer financial law consistently for the purpose of ensuring that all consumers have access to markets for consumer financial products and services and that markets for consumer financial products and services are fair, transparent, and competitive.[54]

The Bureau is established within the FRS, but it has a considerable amount of independence from the FRB. For instance, the FRB does not have the formal authority to stop, delay, or disapprove of a Bureau regulation, nor can it

> a) intervene in any matter or proceeding before the Director [of the CFPB], including examinations or enforcement actions, unless otherwise specifically provided by law;
> b) appoint, direct, or remove any officer or employee of the Bureau; or
> c) merge or consolidate the Bureau, or any of the functions or responsibilities of the Bureau, with any division or office of the Board of Governors or the Federal reserve banks.[55]

The Bureau's authorities are concentrated within a single Director, rather than in a board or commission. The Director is to be appointed by the President, subject to the advice and consent of the Senate, to serve for a five-year term from which he could only be removed for "inefficiency, neglect of duty or malfeasance in office."[56] The Director has authority to hire the employees necessary to carry out the duties of the Bureau[57] and to delegate powers to employees.[58] This structure insulates the Bureau from the Office of the President and allows the Director to steer the course of the CFPB.[59] The Bureau's structure is similar to that of the OCC, which is established within the Department of the Treasury and is headed by a single individual, the Comptroller of the Currency.[60]

The law requires the Director to establish units within the Bureau to focus on consumer financial research; to provide guidance and technical assistance to traditionally underserved areas and individuals; and to monitor and to respond to consumer complaints.

The act also requires the establishment of an Office of Fair Lending and Equal Opportunity; an Office of Financial Education; an Office of Service Member Affairs directed toward members of the military and their families; an Office of Financial Protection for Older Americans to, among other things, "facilitate the financial literacy of individuals who have attained the age of 62 years or more ... on protection from unfair, deceptive, and abusive practices on current and future financial choices";[61] and a Private Education Loan Ombudsman to, among other things, study and attempt to resolve complaints raised by private education loan borrowers.[62]

## General Powers

The authorities of the Bureau fall into three broad categories: supervisory, which includes the power to examine and to impose reporting requirements on financial institutions; enforcement of various consumer protection laws and regulations; and rulemaking. Some of these powers are newly established by the Dodd-Frank Act, such as the authority to supervise nondepository financial institutions.

A significant portion of the Bureau's powers were transferred from other regulators to the Bureau, including the authority to prescribe regulations under the enumerated consumer laws.

## Covered Entities and Activities

Under the CFP Act, the Bureau has authority over an array of consumer financial products and services, including deposit taking, mortgages, credit cards and other extensions of credit, loan servicing, check guaranteeing, collection of consumer report data, debt collection associated with consumer financial products and services, real estate settlement, money transmitting, financial data processing, and others.[63] While the breadth of the products, services, and entities that fall within the Bureau's jurisdiction is considerable, the CFP Act imposes some important exceptions to and limitations on the CFPB's rulemaking, enforcement, and supervisory powers. In some instances, the CFP Act clearly defines the institutions that the Bureau may regulate.[64] In other cases, the statutory language establishes less objective standards that provide the CFPB a fair amount of discretion to determine the types of institutions that may fall within its regulatory jurisdiction.[65] How the Bureau interprets and applies these standards could significantly affect the scope of the Bureau's powers and the impact that the Bureau's actions have on consumer financial markets.

### *Depositories with More Than $10 Billion in Assets*

As is described in greater detail above,[66] the banking regulators traditionally have regulated the depository institutions under their jurisdictions for both safety and soundness and consumer compliance. The CFP Act significantly departs from this traditional model with respect to depository institutions holding more than $10 billion in assets ("larger depositories"). The CFP Act transfers from the banking regulators to the Bureau the primary consumer compliance supervisory, enforcement, and rulemaking authority over larger depositories.[67] The safety and soundness supervisory, enforcement, and rulemaking authority over these institutions remains with their banking regulators (i.e., the OCC, FRB, FDIC, or NCUA).

The Bureau's supervisory powers include the authority to examine larger depositories for consumer compliance, meaning that the CFPB has visitorial[68] powers over larger depositories that historically have been almost exclusively held by their prudential banking regulators. The CFP Act, however, does require the Bureau to coordinate examinations and other supervisory activities with larger depositories' state and federal prudential regulators, and it establishes a procedure for resolving conflicts between the Bureau and a prudential regulator.[69] Furthermore, the Bureau may require reports directly from larger depositories, although it will have to rely on existing reports "to the fullest extent possible."[70]

As a supervisor, the Bureau has an important responsibility of safeguarding non-public information of financial institutions. Through the exercise of its examination and reporting powers, the CFPB (much like banking regulators) may acquire sensitive competitive, commercial, and personal information, as well as evidence of practices that may violate state or federal law. This information could be useful to private litigants, state attorneys general, and market competitors. However, the banking regulators have long protected much of this information from being shared with third parties so as to encourage bank officials to openly provide information without the fear of private lawsuits and to maintain a competitive marketplace.[71] This information also is exempt from public disclosure under the Freedom of Information Act.[72] As a result, parties without examination and other supervisory powers generally have only been able to gain access to proprietary and confidential bank information through litigation.[73] Rules of procedure and evidence associated with litigation serve as significant barriers to access of banks' non-public information, and stand in stark contrast to the supervisory powers of the banking regulators and now the CFPB.

In 2011, the Bureau issued rules that govern how it will handle confidential information acquired through its regulatory actions and the extent to which that information may be shared with individuals and state and federal regulators outside of the CFPB.[74] These rules are very similar, though not identical, to analogous rules prescribed by the banking regulators.[75] Despite their similarity with existing confidentiality rules of the banking regulators, some have expressed concern that the CFPB will be more willing to share non-public bank information, especially with state attorneys general to aid investigations and enforcement actions.[76] These concerns seem to be stoked by at least a couple of issues. One is that the CFPB may exercise its supervisory and enforcement powers over larger depositories with a primary statutory focus on consumer compliance, rather than concentrating on the impact that such actions may have on the institutions' safety and soundness.[77] The second is the Bureau has actively pursued partnerships with state attorneys general as a means to enhance consumer protection.[78] For example, the CFPB and the Presidential Initiative Working Group of the National Association of Attorneys General announced a Joint Statement of Principles, in which they agreed to, among other things,

- Share information, data, and analysis about conduct and practices in the markets for consumer financial products or services to inform enforcement policies and priorities;
- Engage in regular consultation to identify mutual enforcement priorities that will ensure effective and consistent enforcement of the laws that protect consumers of financial products or services;
- Support each other, to the fullest extent permitted by law as warranted by the circumstances, in the enforcement of the laws that protect consumers of financial products or services, including by joint or coordinated investigations of wrongdoing and coordinated enforcement actions; [and]
- Pursue legal remedies to foster transparency, competition, and fairness in the markets for consumer financial products or services across state lines and without regard to corporate forms or charter choice for those providers who compete directly with one another in the same markets;....[79]

Only time will tell whether the Bureau will handle confidential information in much the same way as banking regulators have in the past or whether it will share information with state prosecutors or other third parties more freely.

***Depositories with $10 Billion or Less in Assets***

The Bureau's supervisory and enforcement authority over depositories with $10 billion or less in assets (smaller depository institutions) is far more limited than its powers over larger depositories. The CFP Act does not transfer the primary consumer protection supervisory or enforcement powers over smaller depository institutions to the CFPB; those authorities remain with the prudential banking regulators.

However, the Bureau does have some limited back-up supervisory authority over smaller depository institutions. For instance, the Bureau, "on a sampling basis," may participate in examinations of smaller depository institutions that are conducted by prudential regulators.[80] The prudential regulators must provide the CFPB access to all reports, records, and other documents connected to the examination; must allow the CFPB examiners to participate in all aspects of the examination; and generally must take into account any input that the CFPB's examiner offers regarding the examination. Also, the Bureau may require reports directly from these depositories, although the Bureau will have to rely on existing reports "to the fullest extent possible."[81]

The CFP Act does not provide the Bureau enforcement powers over smaller depository institutions, although the new law does establish a formal procedure by which the Bureau can refer potential enforcement actions against smaller depository institutions to their prudential regulators. The relevant banking regulator would have to respond to the referral but would not be bound to take any other substantive steps associated with it.[82]

Smaller depositories generally will be subject to the consumer protection rules that are prescribed by the Bureau.

***Nondepository Financial Institutions***

The CFP Act does not provide the Bureau with jurisdiction over all nondepository financial institutions. Rather, the CFP Act authorizes the CFPB to regulate providers of three explicit categories of consumer financial products and services, as well as entities that meet one of two discretionary standards. The act explicitly provides the Bureau authority over providers of private student loans, providers of payday loans,[83] and entities that engage in mortgage-related activities, such as mortgage origination, brokerage, mortgage servicing, mortgage modification, and foreclosure relief activities.[84]

The two more flexible standards include any entity that the Bureau considers to be a "larger participant in a [consumer financial] market,"[85] as well as any entity that the Bureau has reasonable cause to believe is "engaging, or has engaged, in conduct that poses risks to consumers with regard to the offering or provision of consumer financial products or services." [86] Rather than rigidly constraining the Bureau's authority to an exhaustive list of institutions and activities, these flexible standards may provide the Bureau the latitude to evolve with the markets by, for example, making it possible to regulate entities that offer consumer financial products or services were not in the marketplace when the Dodd-Frank Act was signed into law. On the other hand, this discretion could create uncertainty for those nondepository financial institutions that do not clearly fall within one of these categories. Concerns associated with this uncertainty might be alleviated if, for example, the CFPB establishes a policy of providing a considerable amount of time between the date on which an institution is determined to be subject to the Bureau's supervision and the date on which such an entity will be directly impacted by the supervision.

The Bureau has the authority to require any company that falls into one of these categories (a "covered nondepository") to register with the Bureau, to submit to examinations, to submit to background checks, and to adhere to other measures designed "to ensure that such persons are legitimate entities and are able to perform their obligations to consumers."[87] However, the Bureau generally must coordinate examinations with any other state and federal regulators that have supervisory authority over covered nondepositories and must rely on existing reports required by those regulators "to the fullest extent possible." The Bureau generally shall serve as the primary enforcer of federal consumer financial laws with respect to covered nondepositories and has primary consumer protection rulemaking authority over such entities.

As previously mentioned, covered nondepositories historically have not been subject to up-front supervision at the federal level. As result, the Bureau's examination, reporting, and other supervisory powers over covered nondepository financial institutions is a significant change from past federal regulation that largely took the form of *ex post* enforcement. These powers give the CFPB the potential to regulate covered nondepositories in an analogous fashion to banks, thrifts, and credit unions. In so doing, the Bureau potentially could eliminate the competitive forces between depositories, nondepositories, and their regulators that some believe led to the "regulatory arbitrage" and "race-to-the-bottom" problems discussed above.

### *Nondepository Institutions with Explicit Exemptions*

The Dodd-Frank Act explicitly exempts a number of entities from the CFPB's jurisdictional reach, such as automobile dealers and accountants. However, the statutory language defining the scope of several of these exemptions is complex and includes subjective standards, such as "regularly extends" and "engaged significantly," that the Bureau might decide to expound on in future guidance and regulations.

## Merchants, Retailers, and Sellers of Nonfinancial Goods and Services

For example, the Bureau generally does not have authority to regulate merchants, retailers, and sellers of non-financial goods and services, even if such an entity extends credit to borrowers for the purchase of their goods and services.[88] However, these entities could engage in certain business practices that would trigger CFPB regulatory authority.

The CFPB could regulate a merchant, retailer, and seller of nonfinancial goods or services if such an entity "regularly extends credit and the credit is subject to a finance charge" and is "engaged significantly in offering or providing consumer financial products or services."[89] Such an entity also could become subject to the CFPB's regulatory authority if it either (1) "assigns, sells or otherwise conveys to another person such [nondelinquent] debt owed by a consumer," or (2) extends credit that "significantly exceeds the market value of the nonfinancial good or service provided" or otherwise evades the CFP Act.[90] However, the Bureau's rulemaking, supervisory, and enforcement authorities are further constrained over certain small businesses, as established by the Small Business Act,[91] that otherwise would only fall under the Bureau's jurisdiction because they "regularly extend[] credit and the credit is subject to a finance charge."[92] For example, a large furniture store with a national presence that occasionally allows customers to pay off the purchase of a bedroom set over the course of 12 months without additional charge, likely would not fall within the Bureau's jurisdictional reach. If that same furniture store charges interest over the 12 months, it is possible that the store could be regulated by the CFPB. However, a small, independently owned furniture store that regularly charges interest on furniture purchases that are paid off over 12 months may fall outside the Bureau's regulatory authority due to the CFP Act's exception for certain small businesses.

The Bureau also has authority over merchants, retailers, and sellers of nonfinancial goods or services to the extent that they fall within the ambit of an enumerated consumer law.[93]

In short, the Bureau's authority to supervise, prescribe regulations, and enforce consumer protection laws on merchants, retailers, and sellers of nonfinancial goods is limited, but not insubstantial. The extent to which the Bureau may regulate these institutions is based on subjective standards such as "regularly extends credit," "engaged significantly," and "significantly exceeds." Unless the Bureau provides greater guidance on how this language will be interpreted, merchants, retailers, and sellers may have difficulty determining whether or not they will be regulated by the CFPB and the extent to which they would have to modify their business practices and procedures to avoid regulation.

**Automobile Dealers**

The Bureau generally does not have supervisory, rulemaking, or enforcement powers over automobile dealers engaged in leasing, selling, or servicing automobiles. However, the Bureau may regulate financial activities engaged in by automobile dealers that are outside of the normal automobile dealer business. For example, the Bureau could regulate an automobile dealer to the extent that it extends credit directly to consumers rather than "routinely assign[ing the credit] to an unaffiliated third party finance or leasing source."[94]

The CFPB also would have jurisdiction over automobile dealers that sell or offer to sell consumer financial products or services unrelated "to the sale, financing, leasing, rental, repair, refurbishment, maintenance, or other servicing of motor vehicles, motor vehicle parts, or any related or ancillary product or services."[95] This could include dealers that offer car title loans, payday loans, or mortgage-related products or services.

Although the Bureau's regulatory powers over automobile dealers are significantly constrained, the CFP Act streamlines the rulemaking process that the FTC must follow to issue unfair or deceptive trade practice rules against automobile dealers. Normally, when the FTC promulgates unfair or deceptive rules pursuant to Section 5 of the Federal Trade Commission Act (FTC Act),[96] it must adhere to the rigorous procedures of the Magnuson-Moss Act,[97] which include public hearings and publishing staff reports.[98] The CFP Act allows the FTC to issue these rules in accordance with the standard informal rulemaking procedures of the Administrative Procedure Act.[99] Thus, while automobile dealers generally are outside of the Bureau's authority, the CFP Act may make it somewhat easier for the FTC to regulate them.

**Other Excluded Entities**

The CFP Act also generally excludes from the Bureau's rulemaking, supervisory, and enforcement authority real estate brokers,[100] real estate agents,[101] sellers of manufactured and mobile homes,[102] income tax preparers,[103] and accountants[104] to the extent that they are acting in their normal capacity (e.g., a real estate broker is exempt to the extent that she brings parties together to purchase a property). However, the CFP Act authorizes some authority for the Bureau to regulate these entities if they extend credit; otherwise sell or offer to sell a consumer financial product or service; or engage in an activity that makes them subject to an enumerated consumer law.

Attorneys generally are exempt from the Bureau's supervisory and enforcement authority (although the act does not explicitly exempt attorneys from the Bureau's rulemaking authority) when they are practicing law. However, this exemption would not apply to the extent that an attorney sells or offers to sell "a consumer financial product or service ... that is not offered or provided as part of, or incidental to, the practice of law, occurring exclusively within the scope of the attorney-client relationship; or that is otherwise offered or provided by the attorney in question with respect to any consumer who is not receiving legal advice or services from the attorney in connection with such financial product or service."[105] Thus, the CFPB likely would not have authority to regulate an attorney who regularly extends financing to her clients explicitly for payment of legal services the attorney provided those clients. Additionally, the Bureau likely would not have authority to regulate an attorney who advances credit based on an expected legal settlement award to a client to buy a car if the attorney were hired in relation to the traffic accident that prompted the need for a new car. However, the CFPB likely could regulate an attorney who regularly converts structured legal settlements to lump sum payments for non-clients.

Other entities and activities that generally fall outside of the Bureau's jurisdictional reach include insurance companies;[106] employee benefit plans;[107] entities that are regulated by state securities commissions;[108] firms regulated by the Securities and Exchange Commission (SEC)[109] or the Commodity Futures Trading Commission (CFTC);[110] those regulated by the Farm Credit Administration;[111] and donations to tax-exempt charities.[112] The CFP Act also explicitly prohibits the Bureau from imposing interest rate caps (a.k.a., usury limits) on any loan or other extension of credit.[113]

## Newly Established Rulemaking

The Dodd-Frank Act establishes procedures that the Bureau must follow when proposing and prescribing rules, in addition to the notice of proposed rulemaking and comment period procedures required for informal rulemakings under the Administrative Procedure Act and other generally applicable federal administrative laws.[114] The act also imposes additional procedures for specific types of rulemaking (e.g., when declaring certain acts or practices to be unfair or abusive), which are discussed below.

### *General Rulemaking Powers*

The CFP Act authorizes the Bureau to "prescribe rules and issue orders and guidance, as may be necessary or appropriate to enable the Bureau to administer and carry out the purposes and objectives of the Federal consumer financial laws, and to prevent evasions thereof."[115] Before proposing a rule and during the comment period of a proposed rule, the CFPB is required to consult with the "appropriate" financial regulators.[116] The Bureau must address any written objections by the federal prudential regulators when issuing final regulations. Additionally, the CFPB must consider "the potential benefits and costs to consumers and covered persons, including the potential reduction of access by consumers to consumer financial products and services resulting from such rule," as well as the impact the rule would have on smaller depositories and "consumers in rural areas."[117]

Additionally, the CFP Act requires the Bureau to take a number of steps to evaluate the impact that proposed regulations may have on small businesses. More specifically, if the Bureau expects that a proposed rule will have a "significant economic impact on a substantial number of small entities,"[118] then it must offer a written analysis that describes, among other things,

> (A) any projected increase in the cost of credit for small entities; (B) any significant alternatives to the proposed rule which accomplish the stated objectives of applicable statutes and which minimize any increase in the cost of credit for small entities; and (C) advice and recommendations of representatives of small entities relating to issues described in subparagraphs (A) and (B)....[119]

Within five years of any CFPB "significant rule or order" becoming effective and after a public comment period, the Bureau must publish a report assessing the effectiveness of the rule or order.[120] The act does not specify what is to be considered "significant," presumably leaving these determinations to the Bureau.

The CFP Act also transfers to the CFPB rulemaking authority under the enumerated consumer laws.[121] In some instances, the Bureau will share rulemaking powers under the enumerated consumer laws with other financial regulators. For example, the CFPB has primary rulemaking authority under the Electronic Funds Transfer Act, but the FRB has exclusive authority to prescribe regulations to implement the debit interchange fee restrictions of Section 920 of that act, which is commonly referred to as the "Durbin Amendment."[122]

As a check on the Bureau's rulemaking powers, the Financial Stability Oversight Council (FSOC)—which is established under Title III of the Dodd-Frank Act and mainly composed of the federal financial regulators, including the Director of the Bureau[123]—has the ability to set aside or stay a regulation prescribed by the Bureau if the regulation "would put the safety and soundness of the United States banking system or the stability of the financial system of the United States at risk."[124] No other federal financial regulator is subject to a similar executive agency "veto" power, so there are no real analogs to look to for guidance on how frequently this power could be used. Because the FSOC is comprised of the heads of financial regulators with whom the CFPB generally must consult when crafting regulations, the Bureau likely will be aware of concerns of FSOC members about a proposed rule and likely will have the opportunity to allay those concerns before a rule is finalized, which may reduce the probability of the FSOC voting to overturn a rule.

### *Specific Rulemaking Powers*

#### Unfair, Deceptive, or Abusive Acts or Practices

The CFP Act provides the Bureau the authority to prescribe rules declaring acts or practices pertaining to covered consumer financial products or services to be unlawful because they are unfair, deceptive, or abusive. This is a broad mandate that leaves the Bureau with a great deal of discretion to determine how to wield this power, in part, because of the inherent difficulty of objectively defining the terms "unfair," "deceptive," and "abusive." However, the Bureau's unfair, deceptive, and abusive rulemaking authority is very similar to the FTC's mandate under the FTC Act.[125] For example, the statutory language defining "unfairness" under the CFP Act is virtually identical to the FTC Act's standard of unfairness.[126] Thus, while it is not statutorily required to do so, the Bureau might look to the FTC's longstanding interpretation of the FTC Act when prescribing regulations under this new authority, to the extent that doing so also comports with the CFP Act.[127]

Although these two mandates are similar in many ways, there are some important distinctions between them. One is their scope. The Bureau's unfair, deceptive, and abusive authority is limited to consumer financial products and services and to those entities that fall under the Bureau's general regulatory jurisdiction. The FTC's authority applies to a broader universe of "acts or practices in or affecting commerce," as that phrase is defined in 15 U.S.C. Section 45.

A second important distinction is the procedural requirements that must be met before rules can be prescribed. When prescribing rules under Section 1023 of the Dodd-Frank Act, the Bureau must consult with the other federal financial regulators, as appropriate, and otherwise follow the general rulemaking procedures, as described above. The FTC, on the other hand, generally must follow the much more onerous, time consuming, and costly procedures of 15 U.S.C. Section 57a, commonly referred to as "Magnuson-Moss rulemaking" after the law that established them.[128]

Another distinction is the statutory use of the term "abusive." The FTC Act does not explicitly bar "abusive" acts or practices. As a result, the FTC has not provided longstanding guidance and commentary on the term's meaning from which the Bureau could draw.[129] The CFP Act does provide the Bureau statutory guidance on the term's meaning, although this statutory language is somewhat malleable. Under the CFP Act, an abusive act or practice may only be deemed unlawful by regulation if it

> materially interferes with the ability of a consumer to understand a term or condition of a consumer financial product or service; or takes unreasonable advantage of (a) a lack of understanding on the part of the consumer ...; (b) the inability of the consumer to protect the interests of the consumer in selecting or using a consumer financial product or service; or (c) the reasonable reliance by the consumer on a covered person to act in the interests of the consumer.[130]

The terms "materially interferes," "unreasonable advantage," and "reasonable reliance" could provide the Bureau the ability to regulate emerging business practices.

At the same time, however, financial service providers may have to deal with the inherent uncertainty associated with the Bureau's future interpretation of the term "abusive."

### Disclosure Requirements

The Bureau also has the authority to prescribe rules imposing disclosure requirements to help consumers understand the terms, benefits, costs, and risks of financial products and services.

When prescribing these rules, the CFPB must follow the general rulemaking procedures described above and also must "consider the available evidence about consumer awareness, understanding of, and responses to disclosures or communications about the risks, costs, and benefits of consumer financial products or services."[131]

### Rulemakings Initiated by the States

If a majority of states adopt a resolution requesting a new consumer protection regulation under the CFPB's jurisdiction or a change in an existing rule, the Bureau must issue a notice of proposed rulemaking on the subject. Before finalizing such a rule, the Bureau must assess whether or not the final rule will (1) increase consumer protection; (2) create more benefits than costs for consumers; (3) unfairly discriminate against a group of consumers; and (4) "likely [] present an unacceptable safety and soundness risk to insured depository institutions," if such a concern is raised by a prudential regulator. If the Bureau decides not to finalize such a rule, it must publish an explanation of the decision in the Federal Register.[132]

## Rulemaking under the Enumerated Consumer Laws

As previously mentioned, the CFPB acquired authority to prescribe regulations pursuant to a large group of federal consumer protection laws that largely predated the Dodd-Frank Act. Individually, these laws target discrete activities.

Taken as a whole, these enumerated consumer laws govern a broad and diverse set of consumer activities and services including debt collection practices, debit card transfers, overdraft services, consumer leases, mortgage lending, credit card lending, mortgage appraisals, real estate settlement practices, and credit reporting, among others. As a result, the transfer of rulemaking authority under these laws represents a major source of the Bureau's regulatory powers.

Although these consumer laws are predominately disclosure-oriented, they also include various substantive restrictions.[133]

The enumerated consumer laws are the Alternative Mortgage Transaction Parity Act;[134] the Consumer Leasing Act of 1976;[135] the Electronic Funds Transfer Act,[136] except with respect to Section 920;[137] the Equal Credit Opportunity Act;[138] the Fair Credit Billing Act;[139] the Fair Credit Reporting Act,[140] except with respect to Section 615(e) and Section 628;[141] the Homeowners Protection Act of 1998;[142] the Fair Debt Collection Practices Act;[143] subsections (b) through (f) of Section 43 of the Federal Deposit Insurance Act;[144] Section 502 through Section 509 of the Gramm-Leach-Bliley Act,[145] except for Section 505 as it applies to Section 501(b);[146] the Home Mortgage Disclosure Act of 1975;[147] the Home Ownership and Equity Protection Act of 1994;[148] the Real Estate Settlement Procedures Act of 1974;[149] the S.A.F.E. Mortgage Licensing Act of 2008;[150] the Truth in Lending Act (TILA);[151] the Truth in Savings Act;[152] Section 626 of the Omnibus Appropriations Act, 2009;[153] the Interstate Land Sales Full Disclosure Act;[154] and most provisions of the Mortgage Reform and Anti-Predatory Lending Act,[155] which was enacted as Title XIV of the Dodd-Frank Act.

The CFPB has not acquired rulemaking authority over all existing federal consumer protection laws.

For example, the FTC retains its primary rulemaking authority under the FTC Act;[156] the banking regulators continue to hold rulemaking authority pursuant to the Community Reinvestment Act;[157] and HUD maintains its rulemaking authority under the Fair Housing Act.[158]

## FUNDING

The Bureau's primary source of funding is not appropriations, like that of most executive agencies, or assessments on institutions within its regulatory jurisdiction, as is typical of federal banking regulators. Instead, the Bureau primarily is funded by a transfer of non-appropriated funds from the FRS's operating expenses, in an amount "determined by the Director to be reasonably necessary to carry out the authorities of the Bureau," subject to specified caps.[159] The cap will be 10% of the total operating expenses of the FRS for FY2011, 11% for FY2012, and 12% thereafter. The caps are based on the operating expenses as reported in the FRS's annual report for 2009 and are to be adjusted for inflation.[160] As a gauge of how much money this will be, the FRS's operating expenses for FY2009 totaled $4.98 billion, 10% of which is just under $500 million.[161] The statutory caps on the funds that may be transferred to the CFPB give the Bureau less flexibility than the OCC, FDIC, and other banking regulators that are able to increase assessments on the institutions within their jurisdiction to raise revenue, as needed to carry out their responsibilities.[162]

Because it does not rely on appropriations for funding, the Bureau is insulated, to some degree, from the uncertainties inherent to the congressional appropriations process. Congress does have many other ways of exerting influence over and conducting oversight of the Bureau's budget outside of the typical appropriations process. The CFP Act, for example, requires the Bureau to submit semi-annual reports to Congress that provide, among other things, a justification of its budget requests. A minimum of twice each year, the Bureau Director must appear before the Senate Committee on Banking, Housing, and Urban Affairs, the House Committee on Financial Services, and the House Committee on Energy and Commerce.[163] The Bureau also must submit certain financial information for Office of Management and Budget review and is subject to regular audits by the Comptroller General.[164] Of course, Congress could pass legislation that subjects the Bureau's budget to additional congressional scrutiny, including the appropriations process.[165]

In addition to the transfer of funds from the FRS, the act authorizes appropriations if the Director "determine[s] that sums available to the Bureau [as specified by the caps] under this section will not be sufficient to carry out the authorities of the Bureau under Federal consumer financial law for the upcoming year." Upon the Bureau's making such a finding and submitting a report to both the House and Senate Committees on Appropriations, the CFP Act provides authorization for an appropriation of $200 million per year for

FY2010-FY2014.[166] To date, the CFPB has not requested appropriated funds nor have any funds been appropriated to the Bureau.

The act also establishes a Consumer Financial Civil Penalty Fund for civil penalties secured by the Bureau for violations of consumer financial protection laws. The fund is to be used to pay victims of such violations, as well as for financial literacy and consumer education programs.[167]

## CONCLUSION

The CFP Act significantly enhances federal consumer protection regulatory authority over nondepository financial institutions, potentially subjecting them to analogous supervisory, examination, and enforcement standards that have been applicable to depository institutions in the past. The act also transfers to the Bureau much of the consumer compliance authority over larger depositories that previously had been held by banking regulators. Additionally, the Bureau acquired the authority to write rules to implement most federal consumer financial protection laws that previously was held by a number of other federal agencies. Although the powers that the CFPB has at its disposal are largely the same or analogous to those that other federal regulators have held for decades, there is uncertainty in how the Bureau will exercise these broad and flexible authorities, especially in light of its almost exclusive focus on consumer protection.

## End Notes

[1] The Bureau acquired rulemaking authority pursuant to most provisions of the Mortgage Reform and Anti-Predatory Lending Act, which was enacted as Title XIV of the Dodd-Frank Act. Dodd-Frank Act §1400.

[2] Dodd-Frank Act §1002(12), 12 U.S.C. §5481(12).

[3] 15 U.S.C. §§1601, *et seq.*

[4] 12 U.S.C. §§2601, *et seq.*

[5] See, e.g., *Who's Watching the Watchmen? Oversight of the Consumer Financial Protection Bureau, Hearing Before the Subcomm. on TARP, Financial Services and Bailouts of Public and Private Programs of the Comm. on Oversight and Government Reform*, 112th Cong. (2011).

[6] *44 U.S. Sen. to Obama: No Accountability, No Confirmation*, Sen. Richard Shelby, News Release, May 5, 2011, available at http://shelby.senate.gov/public/index.cfm/2011/5/44-u-s-sens-to-obama-no-accountability-no-confirmation.

[7] Designated Transfer Date, 75 Fed. Reg. 57,252 (Sept. 20, 2010).

[8] The FDIC, which administers the Deposit Insurance Fund, also has certain regulatory powers over state and national banks holding FDIC-insured deposits; however, these authorities generally are secondary to the institution's primary federal regulator. See, e.g., 12 U.S.C. §1820.

[9] The Dodd-Frank Act eliminated the OTS and transferred its powers to the OCC, FDIC, FRB, and CFPB.

[10] Heidi Mandanis Schooner, *Consuming Debt: Structuring the Federal Response to Abuses in Consumer Credit*, 18 Loy. Consumer L. Rev. 43, 52-53 (2005).

[11] *Id.* at 50, 54-55.

[12] All depositories generally must be examined at least once every 18 months, but the largest depositories have examiners on-site on a continuous basis. See, e.g., 12 U.S.C. §1820(d).

[13] 12 U.S.C. §§1818 and 1831o.

[14] See, e.g., Office of the Comptroller of the Currency, Comptroller's Handbook for Bank Supervision Process, pp. 46- 47 (2007), available at http://www.occ.gov/publications/publications-by-type/comptrollers-handbook/_pdf/ banksupervisionprocess.pdf; Board of Governors of the Federal Reserve System, Commercial Bank Examination Manual §5040.1 (2011), available at http://federalreserve.gov/boarddocs/supmanual/supervision_cbem.htm. See, also, In re Subpoena Served upon Comptroller of Currency, 967 F.2d 630, 633-634 (D.C. Cir. 1992) (discussing the bank examination privilege: "Bank safety and soundness supervision is an iterative process of comment by the regulators and response by the bank. The success of the supervision therefore depends vitally upon the quality of communication between the regulated banking firm and the bank regulatory agency. This relationship is both extensive and informal. It is extensive in that bank examiners concern themselves with all manner of a bank's affairs: Not only the classification of assets and the review of financial transactions, but also the adequacy of security systems and of internal reporting requirements, and even the quality of managerial personnel are of concern to the examiners. The supervisory relationship is informal in the sense that it calls for adjustment, not adjudication. In the process of comment and response, the bank may agree to change some aspect of its operation or accounting; alternatively, if the bank and the examiners reach impasse, then their dispute may be elevated for resolution at higher levels within the bank regulatory agency. It is the very rare dispute, however, that culminates in any formal action, such as a cease and desist order." (internal citations omitted)).

[15] The FTC also serves as the primary federal regulator for many non-financial commercial enterprises.

[16] Heidi Mandanis Schooner, *Consuming Debt: Structuring the Federal Response to Abuses in Consumer Credit*, 18 Loy. Consumer L. Rev. 43, 56-58 (2005). See also Fed. Trade Comm'n Operating Manual, Ch. 1, available at http://www.ftc.gov/foia/ch01overview.pdf.

[17] 15 U.S.C. §§1601, *et seq.*

[18] 15 U.S.C. §§1691, *et seq.*

[19] 12 U.S.C. §§2601, *et seq.*

[20] 12 U.S.C. §§4301, *et seq.*

[21] 15 U.S.C. §§1692, *et seq.*

[22] Other federal consumer protection laws include the Consumer Leasing Act of 1976 (15 U.S.C. §§1667 *et seq.*), which requires certain disclosures for consumer leases; the Electronic Funds Transfer Act (15 U.S.C. §§1693 *et seq.*), which establishes consumer protections regarding electronic fund transfers; the Fair Credit Billing Act (15 U.S.C. §§1666, *et seq.*), which establishes consumer protections regarding billing errors associated with extensions

of credit; and the Fair Credit Reporting Act (15 U.S.C. §§1681, *et seq.*), which governs consumer credit histories and data collection.

[23] Oren Bar-Gill and Elizabeth Warren, *Making Credit Safer*, 157 U. of Penn. L. Rev. 1, 83-85 (Nov. 2008). The activities and services that are covered by the enumerated consumer laws include debt collection practices; debit card transfers; overdraft services; consumer leases; mortgage lending; credit card lending; mortgage appraisals; real estate settlement practices; and credit reporting.

[24] To a lesser extent, other agencies held rulemaking authority under federal consumer laws. For example, rulemaking authority under RESPA was held by HUD.

[25] Heidi Mandanis Schooner, *Consuming Debt: Structuring the Federal Response to Abuses in Consumer Credit*, 18 Loy. Consumer L. Rev. 43, 56-58 (2005); Oren Bar-Gill and Elizabeth Warren, *Making Credit Safer*, 157 U. of Penn. L. Rev. 1, 86-97 (Nov. 2008).

[26] *Id.* See also Fed. Trade Comm'n Operating Manual, Ch. 1, available at http://www.ftc.gov/foia /ch01overview.pdf.

[27] Oren Bar-Gill and Elizabeth Warren, *Making Credit Safer*, 157 U. of Penn. L. Rev. 1, 94-97 (Nov. 2008).

[28] See, e.g., Heidi Mandanis Schooner, *Consuming Debt: Structuring the Federal Response to Abuses in Consumer Credit*, 18 Loy. Consumer L. Rev. 43, 82 (2005) ("The most sensible approach to correcting the structural defect in the current regime would be to eliminate entirely the federal banking regulators' role in consumer protection. This approach has the potential to enhance both the fairness and the efficiency of the current system. This proposal would create a more fair system because banks and non-banks would be treated alike. This would level the playing field among providers of similar financial services. In addition, this proposal provides many potential efficiencies that derive from the recognition of consumer protection as a distinct regulatory goal from prudential regulation."); Oren Bar-Gill and Elizabeth Warren, *Making Credit Safer*, 157 U. of Penn. L. Rev. 1, 98-100 (Nov. 2008).

[29] *Regulatory Restructuring- Safeguarding Consumer Protection and the Role of the Federal Reserve: Hearing Before the Subcomm. on Domestic Monetary Policy & Tech. of the H. Comm. on Fin. Servs.*, 111th Cong. (2009) (written testimony of Patricia A. McCoy, Director of the Insurance Law Center and George J. and Helen M. England Professor of Law at the University of Connecticut School of Law), available at http://archives. financialservices.house.gov/media/ file/hearings/111/mccoy_house_testimony—hearing—july_16_2009.pdf; Adam J. Levitan, *The Consumer Financial Protection Agency*, The PEW Financial Reform Project Briefing Paper # 3, pp. 6-7 (2009), available at http://www.pewtrusts.org/uploadedFiles/wwwpewtrustsorg/Reports/Financial_Reform/ Pew- Levitan-CFPA.pdf; Oren Bar-Gill and Elizabeth Warren, *Making Credit Safer*, 157 U. of Penn. L. Rev. 1, 82-84 (Nov. 2008).

[30] Adam J. Levitan, *The Consumer Financial Protection Agency*, The PEW Financial Reform Project Briefing Paper # 3, p. 4 (2009), available at http://www.pewtrusts.org/ uploaded Files/wwwpewtrustsorg/Reports/Financial_Reform/PewLevitan-CFPA.pdf; Oren Bar-Gill and Elizabeth Warren, *Making Credit Safer*, 157 U. of Penn. L. Rev. 1, 90 (Nov. 2008); Heidi Mandanis Schooner, *The Role of Central Banks in Bank Supervision in the United States and the United Kingdom*, 28 Brook. J. of Int'l L 411, 427 (2003) ("the Federal Reserve's ... regulatory role remains focused on safety and soundness and not on other goals of financial regulation, such as consumer protection.").

[31] *Regulatory Restructuring- Safeguarding Consumer Protection and the Role of the Federal Reserve: Hearing Before the Subcomm. on Domestic Monetary Policy & Tech. of the H. Comm. on Fin. Servs.*, 111th Cong. (2009) (written testimony of Patricia A. McCoy,

Director of the Insurance Law Center and George J. and Helen M. England Professor of Law at the University of Connecticut School of Law), available at http://archives.financialservices.house.gov/media/ file/hearings/111/mccoy_house_testimony—hearing—july_16_2009.pdf; Adam J. Levitan, *The Consumer Financial Protection Agency*, The PEW Financial Reform Project Briefing Paper # 3, pp. 6-7 (2009), available at http://www.pewtrusts.org/uploadedFiles/wwwpewtrustsorg/Reports/Financial_Reform/ Pew-Levitan-CFPA.pdf; Oren Bar-Gill and Elizabeth Warren, *Making Credit Safer*, 157 U. of Penn. L. Rev. 1, 82-84 (Nov. 2008).

[32] *Id.*

[33] *Regulatory Restructuring- Safeguarding Consumer Protection and the Role of the Federal Reserve: Hearing Before the Subcomm. on Domestic Monetary Policy & Tech. of the H. Comm. on Fin. Servs.*, 111th Cong. (2009) (written testimony of Patricia A. McCoy, Director of the Insurance Law Center and George J. and Helen M. England Professor of Law at the University of Connecticut School of Law), available at http://archives.financialservices.house.gov/media/ file/hearings/111/mccoy_house_testimony—hearing—july_16_2009.pdf; Heidi Mandanis Schooner, *Consuming Debt: Structuring the Federal Response to Abuses in Consumer Credit*, 18 Loy. Consumer L. Rev. 43, 82 (2005).

[34] See, e.g., *Regulatory Restructuring- Safeguarding Consumer Protection and the Role of the Federal Reserve: Hearing Before the Subcomm. on Domestic Monetary Policy & Tech. of the H. Comm. on Fin. Servs.*, 111th Cong. (2009) (written testimony of Patricia A. McCoy, Director of the Insurance Law Center and George J. and Helen M. England Professor of Law at the University of Connecticut School of Law), available at http://archives.financialservices.house.gov/media/file/hearings/111/mccoy_house_testimony—hearing— july_16_2009.pdf ("This dual regulatory system allowed mortgage lender [*sic.*] to play regulators off one another by threatening to change charters. Mortgage lenders are free to operate with or without depository institution charters. Similarly, depository institutions can choose between a state and federal charter and between a thrift charter and a commercial bank charter. Each of these choices allows a lender to change regulators. A lender could escape a strict state law by switching to a federal bank or thrift charter or by shifting its operations to a less regulated state. Similarly, a lender could escape a strict regulator by converting its charter to one with a more accommodating regulator."). See, also, Heidi Mandanis Schooner, *Consuming Debt: Structuring the Federal Response to Abuses in Consumer Credit*, 18 Loy. Consumer L. Rev. 43, 82 (2005). It should be noted, however, that depositories receive benefits that generally are not available to nondepositories, and these benefits may offset the distinctions in regulatory burdens, to some degree. These benefits include federal deposit insurance and access to the Federal Reserve's discount window lending facility. 12 U.S.C. §§1815 (deposit insurance), 343 (discount window).

[35] Dain C. Donelson and David Zaring, *Charter Switching and the Financial Crisis: Evidence from the Office of Thrift Supervision*, pp. 11-18 (Oct. 13, 2009) (unpublished paper for the Illinois Corporate Law Symposium), available at http://www.law.illinois.edu/_shared/ pdfs/thrift%20chartering%20draft%2010%20dz.docx.

[36] *Id.* at 8 ("From 1998-2008, OTS lost a net 45 institutions as more thrifts converted to banks than did banks to thrifts. Moreover, some financial institutions have left the federal system altogether. Between 2000 and 2008, at least 30 financial institutions gave up their federal charters and obtained state charters." (internal citations omitted)). See, also, Oren Bar-Gill and Elizabeth Warren, *Making Credit Safer*, 157 U. of Penn. L. Rev. 1, 82-84 (Nov. 2008).

[37] *The Financial Crisis Inquiry Report*, Fin. Crisis Inquiry Comm'n, p. *xviii*, Jan. 2011, available at http://www.gpo.gov/fdsys/pkg/GPO-FCIC/pdf/GPO-FCIC.pdf; Dain C. Donelson and David Zaring, *Charter Switching and the Financial Crisis: Evidence from the Office of Thrift Supervision*, pp. 4-5 (Oct. 13, 2009) (unpublished paper for the Illinois Corporate Law Symposium), available at http://www.law.illinois.edu/_shared/pdfs/ thrift%20 chartering%20draft%2010%20dz.docx ("We also observe that those institutions that switched their charter to OTS during the period of our study had, because of the way the differences between the bank charter and the thrift charter dissipated over time, probably only did so because they preferred being regulated by OTS, rather than because they preferred the business model legislatively required of thrifts (non-thrifts could pursue that model without any legal deficiency or cost)."); *Regulatory Restructuring- Safeguarding Consumer Protection and the Role of the Federal Reserve: Hearing Before the Subcomm. on Domestic Monetary Policy & Tech. of the H. Comm. on Fin. Servs.*, 111th Cong. (2009) (written testimony of Patricia A. McCoy, Director of the Insurance Law Center and George J. and Helen M. England Professor of Law at the University of Connecticut School of Law), available at http://archives.financialservices.house.gov/media/file/hearings/111/ mccoy_ house_testimony—hearing— july_16_2009.pdf; Adam J. Levitan, *The Consumer Financial Protection Agency*, The PEW Financial Reform Project Briefing Paper # 3, pp. 6-7 (2009), available at http://www.pewtrusts.org/uploadedFiles/wwwpewtrustsorg/Reports/ Financial_ Reform/Pew-Levitan-CFPA.pdf; Oren Bar-Gill and Elizabeth Warren, *Making Credit Safer*, 157 U. of Penn. L. Rev. 1, 93-94 (Nov. 2008).

[38] See, e.g., Oren Bar-Gill and Elizabeth Warren, *Making Credit Safer*, 157 U. of Penn. L. Rev. 1, 93-94 (Nov. 2008) ("The OCC's inaction may also be attributable, at least in part, to its direct financial stake in keeping its bank clients happy. Large national banks fund a significant portion of the OCC's budget. ... By attracting more financial-services companies to incorporate as federally chartered banks under the supervision of the OCC, the agency can expand its influence. Accordingly, the OCC would be reluctant to impose substantial constraints on banks, fearing that such constraints might induce the banks to switch to a competing regulator." (internal citations omitted)). See, also, Adam J. Levitan, *The Consumer Financial Protection Agency*, The PEW Financial Reform Project Briefing Paper # 3, pp. 6-7 (2009), available at http://www.pewtrusts.org/uploadedFiles/wwwpewtrustsorg/ Reports/Financial_Reform/PewLevitan-CFPA.pdf.

[39] At least one scholar believes that "regulatory arbitrage" was the primary reason why Countrywide, N.A., the bank subsidiary of what was once the largest mortgage lender in the country, converted from an OCC-regulated national bank to an OTS-regulated thrift in 2007.See, e.g., *Regulatory Restructuring- Safeguarding Consumer Protection and the Role of the Federal Reserve: Hearing Before the Subcomm. on Domestic Monetary Policy & Tech. of the H. Comm. on Fin. Servs.*, 111th Cong. (2009) (written testimony of Patricia A. McCoy, Director of the Insurance Law Center and George J. and Helen M. England Professor of Law at the University of Connecticut School of Law), available at http://archives.financialservices.house.gov/media/file/hearings/111/mccoy_house_testimon y—hearing— july_16_2009.pdf. After the charter conversion, Countrywide, N.A. became Countrywide, F.S.B. Countrywide Financial Corporation, the parent company of Countrywide, F.S.B., has since been acquired by Bank of America, Corporation. See, the historical bank profile of Countrywide, N.A., available at http://www2.fdic.gov/IDASP/ main_bankfind.asp.

[40] *Regulatory Restructuring- Safeguarding Consumer Protection and the Role of the Federal Reserve: Hearing Before the Subcomm. on Domestic Monetary Policy & Tech. of the H.*

*Comm. on Fin. Servs.*, 111th Cong. (2009) (written testimony of Patricia A. McCoy, Director of the Insurance Law Center and George J. and Helen M. England Professor of Law at the University of Connecticut School of Law), available at http://archives.financialservices.house.gov/media/ file/hearings/111/mccoy_house_testimony—hearing—july_16_2009.pdf; Adam J. Levitan, *The Consumer Financial Protection Agency*, The PEW Financial Reform Project Briefing Paper # 3, pp. 6-7 (2009), available at http://www.pewtrusts.org/uploadedFiles/wwwpewtrustsorg/Reports/Financial_Reform/Pew-Levitan-CFPA.pdf; Oren Bar-Gill and Elizabeth Warren, *Making Credit Safer*, 157 U. of Penn. L. Rev. 1, 98 (Nov. 2008).

41 *Regulatory Restructuring- Safeguarding Consumer Protection and the Role of the Federal Reserve: Hearing Before the Subcomm. on Domestic Monetary Policy & Tech. of the H. Comm. on Fin. Servs.*, 111th Cong. (2009) (written testimony of Patricia A. McCoy, Director of the Insurance Law Center and George J. and Helen M. England Professor of Law at the University of Connecticut School of Law), available at http://archives.financialservices.house.gov/media/ file/hearings/111/mccoy_house_testimony—hearing—july_16_2009.pdf; Adam J. Levitan, *The Consumer Financial Protection Agency*, The PEW Financial Reform Project Briefing Paper # 3, pp. 7-8 (2009), available at http://www.pewtrusts.org/uploadedFiles/wwwpewtrustsorg/Reports/Financial_Reform/Pew-Levitan-CFPA.pdf; Oren Bar-Gill and Elizabeth Warren, *Making Credit Safer*, 157 U. of Penn. L. Rev. 1, 98-100 (Nov. 2008).

42 Adam J. Levitan, *The Consumer Financial Protection Agency*, The PEW Financial Reform Project Briefing Paper # 3, p. 4 (2009), available at http://www.pewtrusts.org/uploadedFiles/wwwpewtrustsorg/Reports/Financial_Reform/PewLevitan-CFPA.pdf; Oren Bar-Gill and Elizabeth Warren, *Making Credit Safer*, 157 U. of Penn. L. Rev. 1, 90 (Nov. 2008); Heidi Mandanis Schooner, *The Role of Central Banks in Bank Supervision in the United States and the United Kingdom*, 28 Brook. J. of Int'l L 411, 427 (2003) ("the Federal Reserve's ... regulatory role remains focused on safety and soundness and not on other goals of financial regulation, such as consumer protection.").

43 *Id.*

44 Adam J. Levitan, *The Consumer Financial Protection Agency*, The PEW Financial Reform Project Briefing Paper # 3, p. 5 (2009), available at http://www.pewtrusts.org/uploadedFiles/wwwpewtrustsorg/Reports/Financial_Reform/PewLevitan-CFPA.pdf.

45 Oren Bar-Gill and Elizabeth Warren, *Making Credit Safer*, 157 U. of Penn. L. Rev. 1, 95-97 (Nov. 2008); Heidi Mandanis Schooner, *Consuming Debt: Structuring the Federal Response to Abuses in Consumer Credit*, 18 Loy. Consumer L. Rev. 43, 56-58 (2005).

46 Oren Bar-Gill and Elizabeth Warren, *Making Credit Safer*, 157 U. of Penn. L. Rev. 1, 95-97 (Nov. 2008); Heidi Mandanis Schooner, *Consuming Debt: Structuring the Federal Response to Abuses in Consumer Credit*, 18 Loy. Consumer L. Rev. 43, 82-83 (2005).

47 Oren Bar-Gill and Elizabeth Warren, *Making Credit Safer*, 157 U. of Penn. L. Rev. 1, 85-86 (Nov. 2008).

48 Heidi Mandanis Schooner, *Consuming Debt: Structuring the Federal Response to Abuses in Consumer Credit*, 18 Loy. Consumer L. Rev. 43, 62-63 (2005).

49 *Id.* at 67-69; Oren Bar-Gill and Elizabeth Warren, *Making Credit Safer*, 157 U. of Penn. L. Rev. 1, 90-94 (Nov. 2008).

50 See, e.g., October 2, 2009, Discussion Draft of the Over-the-Counter Derivatives Markets Act of 2009; September 25, 2009, Discussion Draft of the Consumer Financial Protection Agency Act of 2009 (to be reported as H.R. 3126); H.R. 3763, to amend the Fair Credit Reporting Act to provide for an exclusion from Red Flag Guidelines for certain businesses;

and H.R. 3639, Expedited CARD Reform for Consumers Act of 2009, Markup of the H. Comm. on Fin. Services, 111th Cong. (2009), webcasts available at http://archives.financialservices.house.gov/Hearings/hearingDetails.aspx?NewsID=801.

[51] Sarah Bloom Raskin, Gov., Bd. of Gov. of the Fed. Reserve Sys., *Community Bank Examination and Supervision amid Economic Recovery*, speech at the Maryland Bankers Association First Friday Economic Outlook Forum, Jan. 6, 2012, available at http://www.federalreserve.gov/newsevents/speech/raskin20120106a.pdf; *FDIC Oversight: Examining and Evaluating the Role of the Regulator During the Financial Crisis and Today, Hearing Before the Subcomm. on Fin. Inst. and Consumer Credit of the H. Comm. on Fin. Serv.*, 112th Cong. (2011) (written statement of Sheila C. Bair, Chairman, Fed. Deposit Ins. Corp.), available at http://financialservices.house.gov/UploadedFiles/052611bair.pdf.

[52] See, e.g., Ben S. Bernanke, Chairman, Bd. of Gov. of the Fed. Reserve Sys., *The Financial Crisis and Community Banking*, speech at the Independent Community Bankers of America's National Convention and Techworld, Mar. 20, 2009, available at http://www.federalreserve.gov/newsevents/speech/bernanke20090320a.htm ("Many of you likely are frustrated, and rightfully so, by the impact that the financial crisis and economic downturn has had on your banks, as well as on the reputation of bankers more generally. You may well have built your reputations and institutions through responsible lending and community-focused operations, but nonetheless, you now find yourselves facing higher deposit insurance assessments and increasing public skepticism about the behavior of bankers—outcomes that you perceive were largely caused by the actions of larger financial institutions.")

[53] See, e.g., *44 U.S. Sen. to Obama: No Accountability, No Confirmation*, Sen. Richard Shelby, News Release, May 5, 2011, available at http://shelby.senate.gov/public/index.cfm/2011/5/44-u-s-sens-to-obama-no-accountability-noconfirmation.

[54] Dodd-Frank Act §1021, 12 U.S.C. §5511.

[55] Dodd-Frank Act §1012, 12 U.S.C. §5492. The Chairman of the FRB, however, does serve as a voting member of the Financial Stability Oversight Council (FSOC) that has the authority to stay and overturn certain regulations issued by the Bureau. Dodd-Frank Act §111, 12 U.S.C. §5321(b). For a more detailed discussion of the FSOC's authority over CFPB regulations, see the "General Rulemaking Powers" section of this report.

[56] Dodd-Frank Act §1011, 12 U.S.C. §5491.

[57] Dodd-Frank Act §1013, 12 U.S.C. §5493.

[58] Dodd-Frank Act §1012, 12 U.S.C. §5492.

[59] On January 4, 2012, President Obama appointed Richard Cordray to be the first CFPB Director. Cordray's appointment raises a number of significant legal questions regarding the scope of the President's authority under the Recess Appointments Clause of the U.S. Constitution and the statutory authorities these individuals may exercise, which are discussed in CRS Report R42323, *President Obama's January 4, 2012, Recess Appointments: Legal Issues*, by David H. Carpenter et al.

[60] 12 U.S.C. §1. The Comptroller of the Currency also serves for a five-year term and may be "removed by the President, upon reasons to be communicated by him to the Senate." 12 U.S.C. §2. Other financial regulators that are headed by single directors are the Federal Housing Finance Agency (regulator of Fannie Mae, Freddie Mac, and the Federal Home Loan Banks) (12 U.S.C. §4512) and, the former regulator, OTS (12 U.S.C. §1462a). Other financial regulators are set up as commissions or boards. These include the FDIC (12 U.S.C. §1812), the Securities and Exchange Commission (15 U.S.C. §78d), the FTC (15 U.S.C.

§41), the FRB (12 U.S.C. §241), and the NCUA (12 U.S.C. §1725a). See, also, Senate Report No. 111-176, p. 161 (2010) (explaining that the CFPB's executive and administrative structures "are modeled on similar statutes governing the Office of the Comptroller of the Currency and the Office of Thrift Supervision, which are located within the Department of the Treasury.").

[61] Dodd-Frank Act §1013, 12 U.S.C. §5493.

[62] Dodd-Frank Act §1035, 12 U.S.C. §5535.

[63] Dodd-Frank Act §1002(15), 12 U.S.C. §5481(15). The Bureau also has authority over "service providers," which generally includes individuals that provide "a material service to a covered person in connection with the offering or provision of a consumer financial product or service...." Dodd-Frank Act §1002(26), 12 U.S.C. §5481(26).

[64] E.g., depository institutions holding more than $10 billion in assets. Dodd-Frank Act §1025, 12 U.S.C. §5515.

[65] E.g., nondepository financial institutions that are "larger participant[s] in a market." Dodd-Frank Act §1024, 12 U.S.C. §5514.

[66] See the "Federal Consumer Financial Protection Regulation Before the CFPB" section of this report.

[67] Dodd-Frank Act §§1061-1067, 12 U.S.C. §§5581-5587.

[68] 12 C.F.R. Section 7.4000 defines visitorial powers to include

I. Examination of a bank;
II. Inspection of a bank's books and records;
III. Regulation and supervision of activities authorized or permitted pursuant to federal banking law; and
IV. Enforcing compliance with any applicable Federal or state laws concerning those activities, including through investigations that seek to ascertain compliance through production of nonpublic information by the bank [subject to certain exceptions]....

See, also, Guthrie v. Harkness, 199 U.S. 148, 158 (1905) ("Visitation, in law, is the act of a superior or superintending officer, who visits a corporation to examine into its manner of conducting business, and enforce an observance of its laws and regulations. [Alexander M.] Burrill defines the word to mean 'inspection; superintendence; direction; regulation.'" (Burrill authored legal dictionaries often used at the time of the case.)).

[69] Dodd-Frank Act §1025, 12 U.S.C. §5515.

[70] Dodd-Frank Act §1025, 12 U.S.C. §5515.

[71] See, e.g., 12 C.F.R. §4.36 ("It is the OCC's policy regarding non-public OCC information that such information is confidential and privileged. Accordingly, the OCC will not normally disclose this information to third parties.").

[72] 5 U.S.C. §552(b)(8) (exempting from public disclosure, information "contained in or related to examination, operating, or condition reports prepared by, on behalf of, or for the use of an agency responsible for the regulation or supervision of financial institutions....").

[73] See, generally, CRS Report R40595, *Cuomo v. The Clearing House Association, L.L.C: National Banks Are Subject to State Lawsuits to Enforce Non-Preempted State Laws*, by M. Maureen Murphy.

[74] Disclosure of Records and Information, 76 Fed. Reg. 45,372 (July 28, 2010) (codified at 12 C.F.R. pt. 1070).

[75] E.g., *compare id. with* the OCC's regulations on the release of non-public information, 12 C.F.R. §§4.31-4.40.

[76] See, e.g., Melanie Hibbs Brody, Paul F. Hancock, David G. McDonough, Jr., and Stephanie C. Robinson, *And the Plot Thickens: the CFPB Issues A Quartet of Interim Final Rules Laying Out Its Investigatory and Enforcement Procedures*, Aug. 16, 2011, available at http://www.klgates.com/and-the-plot-thickens-08-16-2011/. A separate area of concern involves the affect that submitting documents to the Bureau as part of the regulatory process will have on the attorney-client and other privileges. For more information on this subject, see Confidential Treatment of Privileged Information, 76 Fed. Reg. 15,286 (Mar. 15, 2012) and the public comments to the proposal.

[77] See, generally, Thomas P. Vartanian, *All You Need to Know About CFPB Exam Is in the Manual*, American Banker, Feb. 13, 2012, available at http://www.americanbanker.com/ bankthink/all-you-need-to-know-about-CFPB-exam-is-inthe-manual-1046629-1.html?zkPrintable=true. Sharing non-public information in some instances may create litigation risk or cause reputational harm that may negatively impact an institution's safety and soundness.

[78] Melanie Hibbs Brody, Paul F. Hancock, David G. McDonough, Jr., and Stephanie C. Robinson, *And the Plot Thickens: the CFPB Issues A Quartet of Interim Final Rules Laying Out Its Investigatory and Enforcement Procedures*, Aug. 16, 2011, available at http://www.klgates.com/and-the-plot-thickens-08-16-2011/.

[79] Consumer Financial Protection Bureau and National Association of Attorneys General Presidential Initiative Working Group Release Joint Statement of Principles, CFPB Press Release, Apr. 11, 2011, available at http://www.consumerfinance.gov/pressrelease/ consumer-financial-protection-bureau-and-national-association-ofattorneys-general-presidential-initiative-working-group-release-joint-statement-of-principles/.

[80] Dodd-Frank Act §1026(c), 12 U.S.C. §5516(c).

[81] Dodd-Frank Act §1026(b), 12 U.S.C. §5516(b).

[82] Dodd-Frank Act §1026(d), 12 U.S.C. §5516(d).

[83] While the Bureau has authority to regulate payday lenders, it does not have authority to set usury limits. Dodd-Frank Act §1027(o), 12 U.S.C. §5517(o). Some consumer advocates have argued that interest rate caps are the only proven way to effectively curb predatory practices of payday lenders. Center for Responsible Lending, *Issue Brief: Payday Loans Put Families in the Red*, Feb. 2009, available at http://www.responsiblelending.org/payday-lending/researchanalysis/payday-puts-families-in-the-red-final.pdf ("Payday lending industry representatives have lobbied for other reforms, such as payment plans and renewal bans, because they understand that these measures have done nothing to slow the rate at which they can flip loans to the same borrowers. But an interest rate cap is the only measure that has proven effective.").

[84] Dodd-Frank Act §1024, 12 U.S.C. §5514.

[85] As determined by the Bureau in regulations after consultation with the FTC. Dodd-Frank Act §1024, 12 U.S.C. §5514.

[86] Dodd-Frank Act §1024, 12 U.S.C. §5514.

[87] Dodd-Frank Act §1024, 12 U.S.C. §5514.

[88] Dodd-Frank Act §1027(a), 12 U.S.C. §5517(a) ("Except as provided in subparagraph (B), and subject to subparagraph (C), the Bureau may not exercise any rulemaking, supervisory, enforcement, or other authority under this title with respect to a merchant, retailer, or seller of nonfinancial goods or services, but only to the extent that such person—(i) extends credit directly to a consumer ... exclusively for the purpose of enabling that consumer to purchase such nonfinancial good or service directly from the merchant, retailer, or seller; (ii) ...

collects debt arising from [such] credit ... or (iii) sells or conveys [such] debt ... that is delinquent or otherwise in default.").

[89] Dodd-Frank Act §1027(a)(2), 12 U.S.C. §5517(a)(2).

[90] Dodd-Frank Act §1027(a)(2), 12 U.S.C. §5517(a)(2).

[91] 15 U.S.C. §632.

[92] Dodd-Frank Act §1027(a)(2)(D), 12 U.S.C. §5517(a)(2)(D). To qualify as a small business for the purposes of this provision, a merchant, retailer, or seller must meet the size thresholds that are provided by 15 U.S.C. §632.

[93] Dodd-Frank Act §1027(a)(1), 12 U.S.C. §5517(a)(1).

[94] Dodd-Frank Act §1029, 12 U.S.C. §5519.

[95] Dodd-Frank Act §1029, 12 U.S.C. §5519.

[96] 15 U.S.C. §45.

[97] 15 U.S.C. §57a.

[98] See, Federal Trade Commission Operating Manual ch. 7.3, available at http://www.ftc.gov/foia/ch07rulemaking.pdf. Other steps include "an investigation oriented towards rulemaking," a staff report that "provide[s] sufficient reason for the Commission to conclude that corrective actions is warranted and that rulemaking is the enforcement method of choice," an advance notice of proposed rulemaking (ANPR) published in the *Federal Register*, making the information collected as part of the investigation available for public review, and publishing a final staff report. See, also, p. 3, note 23, of CRS Report R41546, *A Brief Overview of Rulemaking and Judicial Review*, by Vanessa K. Burrows and Todd Garvey.

[99] 5 U.S.C. §553. See, also, pp. 1-2 of CRS Report R41546, *A Brief Overview of Rulemaking and Judicial Review*, by Vanessa K. Burrows and Todd Garvey.

[100] Dodd-Frank Act §1027(b), 12 U.S.C. §5517(b).

[101] Dodd-Frank Act §1027(b), 12 U.S.C. §5517(b).

[102] Dodd-Frank Act §1027(c), 12 U.S.C. §5517(c).

[103] Dodd-Frank Act §1027(d), 12 U.S.C. §5517(d).

[104] Dodd-Frank Act §1027(d), 12 U.S.C. §5517(d).

[105] Dodd-Frank Act §1027(e), 12 U.S.C. §5517(e).

[106] Dodd-Frank Act §1027(f), 12 U.S.C. §5517(f).

[107] Dodd-Frank Act §1027(g), 12 U.S.C. §5517(g).

[108] Dodd-Frank Act §1027(h), 12 U.S.C. §5517(h).

[109] Dodd-Frank Act §1027(i), 12 U.S.C. §5517(i).

[110] Dodd-Frank Act §1027(j), 12 U.S.C. §5517(j).

[111] Dodd-Frank Act §1027(k), 12 U.S.C. §5517(k).

[112] Dodd-Frank Act §1027(*l*), 12 U.S.C. §5517(*l*).

[113] Dodd-Frank Act §1027(o), 12 U.S.C. §5517(o).

[114] 5 U.S.C. §553. For a more detailed discussion of the Bureau's rulemaking procedural requirements, see CRS Report R41380, *The Dodd-Frank Wall Street Reform and Consumer Protection Act: Regulations to be Issued by the Consumer Financial Protection Bureau*, by Curtis W. Copeland.

[115] Dodd-Frank Act §1022(b), 12 U.S.C. §5512(b).

[116] Dodd-Frank Act §1022(b), 12 U.S.C. §5512(b).

[117] Dodd-Frank Act §1022(b), 12 U.S.C. §5512(b).

[118] "Small entities" include small businesses, small organizations, and small governmental jurisdictions, as those terms are defined at 5 U.S.C. §601.

[119] 5 U.S.C. §603(d), as amended by Dodd-Frank Act §1100G. These requirements would not have to be met if the CFPB issued final regulations without issuing a notice of proposed rulemaking as allowed under certain circumstances pursuant to the Administrative Procedure Act. The Bureau, at times, also must convene an "advocacy review panel" pursuant to the Regulatory Flexibility Act. For a more detailed description of the Bureau's obligations under the Regulatory Flexibility Act, see p. 17 of CRS Report R41380, *The Dodd-Frank Wall Street Reform and Consumer Protection Act: Regulations to be Issued by the Consumer Financial Protection Bureau*, by Curtis W. Copeland.

[120] Dodd-Frank Act §1022(d), 12 U.S.C. §5512(d).

[121] Dodd-Frank Act Title X, Subtitle H, 12 U.S.C. §§5581, *et seq.*

[122] 15 U.S.C. §1693b, as amended by Dodd-Frank Act §1084(3).

[123] The Director also will serve as an ex-officio member of the FDIC board. 12 U.S.C. §1812(f)(2), as amended by Dodd-Frank Act §336.

[124] Dodd-Frank Act §1023(a), 12 U.S.C. §5513(a).

[125] 15 U.S.C. §§41, *et seq.*

[126] *Compare* Dodd-Frank Act §1031, 12 U.S.C. §5531(the Bureau may not declare an act or practice unfair unless it has "a reasonable basis to conclude that the act or practice causes or is likely to cause substantial injury to consumers, which is not reasonably avoidable by consumers; and such substantial injury is not outweighed by countervailing benefits to consumers or competition.") *with* 15 U.S.C. §45(n) ("The [Federal Trade] Commission shall have no authority under this section or section 57a of this title to declare unlawful an act or practice on the grounds that such act or practice is unfair unless the act or practice causes or is likely to cause substantial injury to consumers which is not reasonably avoidable by consumers themselves and not outweighed by countervailing benefits to consumers or to competition.").

[127] See, e.g., FTC Policy Statement on Unfairness, Dec. 17, 1980, available at http://www.ftc.gov/bcp/policystmt/adunfair.htm and FTC Policy Statement on Deception, Oct. 14, 1983, available at http://www.ftc.gov/bcp/policystmt/addecept.htm.

[128] Magnuson-Moss Warranty—Federal Trade Commission Improvement Act, P.L. 93-637, 15 U.S.C. §57a. See, Federal Trade Commission Operating Manual ch. 7.3, available at http://www.ftc.gov/foia/ch07rulemaking.pdf. Required steps include "an investigation oriented towards rulemaking"; a staff report that "provide[s] sufficient reason for the Commission to conclude that corrective actions is warranted and that rulemaking is the enforcement method of choice"; an advance notice of proposed rulemaking (ANPR) published in the *Federal Register*, making the information collected as part of the investigation available for public review; and publishing a final staff report. See, also, p. 3, note 23, of CRS Report R41546, *A Brief Overview of Rulemaking and Judicial Review*, by Vanessa K. Burrows and Todd Garvey. As is discussed above, the FTC does not have to comply with the Magnusson-Moss rulemaking procedures to issue unfair or deceptive trade practice regulations against automobile dealers. Dodd-Frank Act §1029, 12 U.S.C. §5519. Although previous iterations of what would ultimately become the CFP Act modified the FTC's rulemaking procedures for declaring unfair or deceptive trade practices under Section 5 of the FTC Act, those changes were not included in the Dodd-Frank Act, as enacted.

[129] Other federal consumer protection laws under which the FTC historically has held rulemaking and enforcement authority do prohibit "abusive" practices. For example, Section 806 of the Fair Debt Collection Practices Act (15 U.S.C. §§1692, *et seq.*) prohibits debt collectors from engaging in conduct, "the natural consequence of which is to harass, oppress, or *abuse*

any person in connection with the collection of a debt." 15 U.S.C. §1692d (emphasis added). The Telemarketing and Consumer Fraud and Abuse Prevention Act (15 U.S.C. §§6101 *et seq.*) also provides the FTC the authority to "prescribe rules prohibiting deceptive telemarketing acts or practices and other *abusive* telemarketing acts or practices." 15 U.S.C. 6102(a) (emphasis added). As a result, the FTC does have experience interpreting the terms "abuse" and "abusive" in contexts outside of the FTC Act. See, e.g., FTC Staff Commentary on the Fair Debt Collection Practices Act, 53 Fed. Reg. 50,097 (Dec. 13, 1988); 16 C.F.R. §310.4.

[130] Dodd-Frank Act §1031, 12 U.S.C. §5531.

[131] Dodd-Frank Act §1032, 12 U.S.C. §5532.

[132] Dodd-Frank Act §1041(c), 12 U.S.C. §5551(c).

[133] See, e.g., Truth in Lending Act, 73 Fed. Reg. 44,522 (July 30, 2008) (the FRB issued final regulations imposing a number of substantive restrictions on mortgage lending pursuant to the rulemaking authority of TILA §129*l*(2) (15 U.S.C. §1639(*l*)(2)).

[134] 12 U.S.C. §§3801, *et seq.*

[135] 15 U.S.C. §§1667, *et seq.*

[136] 15 U.S.C. §§1693, *et seq.*

[137] Section 920 of the Electronic Funds Transfer Act delineates the interaction between the EFTA and state laws. 15 U.S.C. §1693q.

[138] 15 U.S.C. §§1691, *et seq.*

[139] 15 U.S.C. §§1666, *et seq.*

[140] 15 U.S.C. §§1681, *et seq.*

[141] 15 U.S.C. §§1681m(e) and 1681w. These provisions primarily pertain to "red flag" identity theft prevention measures for federal financial institutions and credit report record retention by federal financial institutions.

[142] 12 U.S.C. §§4901, *et seq.*

[143] 15 U.S.C. §§1692, *et seq.*

[144] 12 U.S.C. §§1831t(c)-(f). These provisions pertain to disclosure requirements for depository institutions that do not hold federal deposit insurance.

[145] 15 U.S.C. §§6802-6809. These provisions deal with financial institutions' use and protection of non-public consumer information.

[146] This provision pertains to federal banking agency rulemaking applicable to the safeguarding of non-public personal information by banking concerns.

[147] 12 U.S.C. §§2801, *et seq.*

[148] 15 U.S.C. §1639.

[149] 12 U.S.C. §§2601, *et seq.*

[150] 12 U.S.C. §§5101, *et seq.*

[151] 15 U.S.C. §§1601, *et seq.*

[152] 12 U.S.C. §§4301, *et seq.*

[153] P.L. 111-8, §626. This provision pertains to a regulation under which states may bring actions to enforce certain Truth in Lending Act requirements regarding mortgage loans.

[154] 15 U.S.C. §§1701, *et seq.*

[155] Dodd-Frank Act Title XIV, Subtitles A, B, C, and E, and §§1471, 1472, 1475, and 1476. See Dodd-Frank Act §1400.

[156] 15 U.S.C. §§41, *et seq.*

[157] 12 U.S.C. §§2901, *et seq.*

[158] 42 U.S.C. §§3601, *et seq.*

159 Dodd-Frank Act §1017, 12 U.S.C. §5497.

[160] Dodd-Frank Act §1017, 12 U.S.C. §5497.

[161] Federal Reserve System's 96th Annual Report, 2009, available at http://www.federal reserve.gov/boarddocs/ rptcongress/annual09/pdf/AR09.pdf.

[162] See, e.g., 12 U.S.C. §§482, 1817(b).

[163] Dodd-Frank Act §1016, 12 U.S.C. §5496.

[164] Dodd-Frank Act §1017(a), 12 U.S.C. §5497(a); P.L. 112-10 §1573(c), 12 U.S.C. §5496a.

[165] H.R. 2434, the Financial Services and General Government Appropriations Act, 2012, for example, would require the CFPB to be funded through appropriations after FY2012.

[166] Dodd-Frank Act §1017(e), 12 U.S.C. §5497(e).

[167] Dodd-Frank Act §1017(b), 12 U.S.C. §5497(b).

In: The Consumer Financial Protection Bureau ISBN 978-1-62257-637-1
Editors: P. J. Cerutti and M. Kolchak 

*Chapter 2*

# REVISITING MORTGAGE LOAN DISCLOSURES UNDER THE CONSUMER FINANCIAL PROTECTION BUREAU*

***Darryl E. Getter and Sean M. Hoskins***

## SUMMARY

High default and foreclosure rates in the housing market have resulted in questions as to whether borrowers were fully informed about the terms of their mortgage loans. A lack of transparency with respect to loan terms and settlement costs can make it difficult for consumers to make well-informed decisions when choosing mortgage products. In addition, inadequate disclosures can make some borrowers more vulnerable to predatory lending or discriminatory practices.

The adequate disclosure of mortgage terms is a longstanding issue that has prompted several congressional actions. For example, the Truth in Lending Act (TILA) of 1968 and the Real Estate Settlement Procedures Act (RESPA) of 1974 were enacted to require disclosures of credit costs and terms to borrowers. The Economic Growth and Regulatory Paperwork Reduction Act of 1996 (P.L. 104-208) directed the Federal Reserve Board and the Department of Housing and Urban Development (HUD) to propose a single form that satisfied the requirements of RESPA and TILA. However, the Federal Reserve Board

* This is an edited, reformatted and augmented version of Congressional Research Service, Publication No. R41980, dated June 6, 2012.

and HUD concluded that regulatory changes would not be sufficient and that further statutory changes would be required for the forms to be consolidated. More recently, the Dodd-Frank Wall Street Reform and Consumer Protection Act of 2010 (Dodd-Frank Act; P.L. 111-203), which established the Consumer Financial Protection Bureau (CFPB), mandated the new agency revisit disclosure stipulations for mortgage loans. In addition, the Dodd-Frank Act requires the CFPB to consolidate mandatory TILA and RESPA disclosures into one Loan Estimate form.

The 112th Congress has been closely monitoring the subsequent rulemaking associated with the Dodd-Frank Act, as well as the performance and effectiveness of the CFPB. Consequently, this report examines one of the first major actions undertaken by the new agency. Specifically, efforts by the CFPB to create an effective mortgage disclosure form for borrowers are discussed.

## INTRODUCTION

Relatively high default and foreclosure rates in the housing market have led some to question whether borrowers were fully informed about the terms of their mortgage loans. There has been concern that mortgage disclosure forms are confusing and not easily understood by borrowers. It has been argued that transparent mortgage terms could enhance consumer shopping and discourage predatory, discriminatory, and fraudulent lending practices. Lending practices that involve hidden costs may result in a payment shock to a borrower, possibly leading to financial distress or even foreclosure.

The issue of adequate disclosure of mortgage terms is longstanding. The Truth in Lending Act (TILA) of 1968, which was previously implemented by the Federal Reserve Board via Regulation Z,[1] requires lenders to disclose the cost of credit and repayment terms of mortgage loans before borrowers enter into any transactions.[2] The TILA Disclosure Statement conveys information about the credit costs and terms of the transaction. The TILA Disclosure Statement lists the annual percentage rate (APR), an interest rate calculation that incorporates both the loan rate and fees. The statement also discloses finance charges, the amount financed, the total number of the payments, whether the interest rate on the mortgage loan can change, and whether the borrower has the option to refinance the loan.

The Real Estate Settlement Procedures Act (RESPA) of 1974 is another element of the consumer disclosure regime. RESPA requires standardized disclosures about the settlement or closing costs, which are costs associated with the acquisition of residential mortgages.[3] Examples of such costs include loan origination fees or points, credit report fees, property appraisal fees, mortgage insurance fees, title insurance fees, home and flood insurance fees, recording fees, attorney fees, and escrow account deposits. In other words, the mortgage loan rate and fees are disclosed in separate calculations rather than in one calculation.

In addition, RESPA, which was implemented by the Department of Housing and Urban Development (HUD),[4] includes the following provisions: (1) providers of settlement services are required to provide a good faith estimate (GFE) of the settlement service costs borrowers should expect at the closing of their mortgage loans;[5] (2) a list of the actual closing costs must be provided to borrowers at the time of closing, which are typically listed on the HUD-1 settlement statement; and (3) RESPA prohibits "referral fees" or "kickbacks" among settlement service providers to prevent settlement fees from increasing unnecessarily.

The Dodd-Frank Wall Street Reform and Consumer Protection Act of 2010 (Dodd-Frank Act; P.L. 111-203) transferred general rulemaking authority for various provisions of TILA and RESPA to a new Consumer Financial Protection Bureau (CFPB)[6] effective July 21, 2011.[7] Lenders currently present borrowers with both TILA and RESPA disclosures, but the Dodd-Frank Act has directed the CFPB to create a single disclosure form that satisfies both disclosure requirements.[8] The CFPB must issue a proposed rule of the new Loan Estimate form within one year of its July 21, 2011 transfer date.[9] The CFPB released two initial Loan Estimate prototypes in May 2011 and has proposed several rounds of updated prototypes since then.[10] This report reviews current efforts to regulate the reporting of pertinent loan information to consumers, including actions taken by the CFPB.[11]

## 2008 Disclosure Modifications

As previously stated, TILA requires mortgage lenders to present borrowers with a disclosure statement that conveys information about the credit costs and terms of the transaction in one APR calculation expressed as a percentage. TILA was amended in 1980 to require the Federal Reserve to publish APR disclosure forms.[12] On November 17, 2008, HUD made changes to the RESPA component of the mortgage disclosure process that it supervises.[13] Key modifications are discussed below.

## Standardizing the Good Faith Estimate Form

HUD's final rule developed a standardized good faith estimate form for use in the initial stages of obtaining mortgages.[14] The GFE included changes intended to help consumers better understand and locate relevant information about their mortgage products. For example, the GFE conveys information about the mortgage terms, whether the interest rate can rise, whether the overall loan balance can rise, whether the loan has a prepayment penalty, whether the loan has a balloon payment, and whether the quoted monthly payment includes a monthly escrow payment for taxes. All of this information about the loan appears on the first page of the GFE.

In addition to facilitating comparison shopping, the HUD GFE form also results in reliable GFEs in the sense that some of the estimated costs are required to not change substantially by the time consumers are ready to close on their loans. Shopping for the best deal or the most affordable loan would be pointless if the costs were to change when borrowers arrived at closing. Consequently, page three of the GFE lists charges that cannot increase, charges that are allowed to increase up to 10%, and charges that may change at settlement. For specific charges that should not change or exceed the 10% limit, a borrower has the option to withdraw the application. This makes it difficult for lenders to generate "costs" or fees that could not be easily justified.

A separate GFE is required for each loan product offered to the borrower. For example, a borrower may wish to compare a traditional fixed rate mortgage (FRM) loan with an adjustable rate mortgage (ARM) loan. Both mortgage products must have separate GFEs to ensure that the information provided is unique to each product. HUD argued that these changes to the GFE would reduce confusion about loan and settlement costs, help the borrower better determine product affordability, and facilitate comparison shopping.[15]

HUD distinguished two stages in the overall mortgage seeking process.[16] The consumer receives a GFE in stage 1, which occurs prior to proceeding with the official mortgage application in stage 2. In the first stage, the lender is not expected to have performed any underwriting, and the GFE need only consist of information obtained from the borrower without any verification of borrower statements. Final underwriting is expected to begin in stage 2 after the borrower has expressed a willingness to proceed with an official mortgage application. The GFE becomes binding only if the underwriting process confirms borrower statements and loan qualifications. If the underwriting process reveals that the borrower is unable to qualify for the specific loan product, then the lender may reject the borrower or propose a new GFE for another loan product in which the borrower is more likely to qualify.

The TILA Disclosure Statement also has a two-stage process similar to the GFE. If the initial APR on the disclosure changes by more than a certain amount after the loan underwriting is performed, the lender must provide a corrected Disclosure Statement at least three days before the loan can be finalized. If a term other than the APR changes after underwriting, then the corrected disclosure must be presented to the borrower at the time the loan is finalized.[17]

For a majority of prime or high-credit quality borrowers, the final loan rates initially stated on the GFE forms are likely to become the actual ones after underwriting. Lenders typically advertise the interest rates that prime borrowers are likely to be charged, and high-credit quality borrowers are arguably already able to shop for loans.[18] Subprime or high-risk borrowers, however, encounter difficulties shopping for loan rates and may continue to do so under this system. Lenders typically charge higher rates to riskier borrowers to compensate for the additional risk, and such rates are typically determined after underwriting has occurred. Hence, low-credit quality borrowers may be less likely to obtain estimates of loan rates prior to final underwriting that would not change afterwards. Assuming no substantial shifts in the current proportion of prime relative to subprime borrowers, or that the share of prime borrowers diminishes as a result of further borrower risk gradations, underwriting at the GFE stage might not be necessary for the vast majority of consumers to obtain fairly reliable pricing information of mortgage products.

A standardized HUD-1 settlement statement is required at all settlements or closings involving mortgage loans. The HUD-1 lists all settlement charges paid at closing, the seller's net proceeds, and the buyer's net payment. HUD modified the HUD-1 form to make it easier for borrowers to trace the estimated costs on the GFE to the actual charges listed on the HUD-1 form. The itemized charges listed on the HUD-1 form include references to the same charges originally listed on the GFE. With these references, it may become more apparent to borrowers what charges remained the same or changed from the estimation stage to the closing stage.

## Disclosure of Yield Spread Premium and the Trade-off Table

Prior to implementation of the standardized GFE, a Federal Trade Commission (FTC) study tested 819 consumers to document their understanding of mortgage cost disclosures and loan terms, as well as their ability to avoid deceptive lending practices.[19] The authors found that both prime and subprime borrowers had difficulty understanding important mortgage costs after viewing mortgage cost disclosures. Some borrowers had difficulty identifying the APR of the loan and loan amounts. Many borrowers did not understand why the interest rate and APR of a loan would differ.[20] In addition, borrowers had trouble understanding loan terms for the more complicated mortgage products, such as those with optional credit insurance, interest-only payments, balloon payments, and prepayment penalties. Many borrowers were unable to determine whether balloon payments, prepayment penalties, or up-front loan charges were part of the loan.

The inability to understand a loan offer makes a borrower more vulnerable to predatory lending. Predatory loans are often characterized by high fees or interest rates and other provisions that may not benefit the borrower.[21] Given that one area particularly susceptible to predatory action is the calculation of lender compensation, HUD's revised GFE form includes new disclosure methods so borrowers can understand the fees they are charged to obtain their mortgage loans. Loan charges may be collected either through points (up-front fees), or via the interest rate mechanism, which is referred to as the yield spread premium (YSP), or some combination of these two pricing mechanisms.[22] Page two of the revised standardized GFE form discloses the computation of the total origination costs.[23]

In addition, if borrowers realize that mortgage loan origination costs may be collected by some combination of up-front fees and YSP, then they may also realize that it is possible to choose between paying higher up-front fees for a lower interest rate or lower up-front fees for a higher interest rate. Recognition of this trade-off may help borrowers avoid being charged both higher rates and higher fees. The GFE includes a trade-off table on page three to facilitate the understanding of the trade-off between interest rates and points. The trade-off table discloses how a loan with the same principal face value and a lower interest rate results in higher up-front settlement costs; it also discloses how the same loan with a higher interest rate results in lower up-front settlement costs.

Although the trade-off table was found to benefit consumers,[24] HUD's final rule required only the leftmost column of the table to be filled out. The decision to allow loan originators the option to fill out the remaining columns was related to concerns regarding the cost burden and time to calculate comparable loan costs information.[25] In addition, the trade-off table may still be difficult to interpret for loans with adjustable interest rates, which are likely to change over the life of the loan and distort the inverse relationship between the interest rate and up-front fees. Some borrowers, however, may be inclined to request that loan originators fill out the table completely, which would facilitate HUD's policy objectives to achieve transparency.[26]

## RECENT CFPB PROPOSALS

As required by the Dodd-Frank Act, the CFPB has proposed various prototypes of a standardized Loan Estimate form to combine the TILA Disclosure Statement and HUD's GFE into a single document.[27] The Dodd-Frank Act directed the CFPB to issue a proposed rule of the new Loan Estimate form within one year of its July 21, 2011 transfer date.[28] The CFPB stated its plans to perform five rounds of testing in six different cities before the final rule is proposed.[29] In addition to consumer testing, the CFPB also stated that it will convene a Small Business Review Panel to solicit feedback on its prototype.[30] The current prototype, Tupelo, is the most recent form available on the CFPB website and has been developed after at least five rounds of testing.[31]

Tupelo has three pages with the first page containing three sections.[32] The first section presents the loan amount; the interest rate and whether it can change; the monthly loan payment; and whether a prepayment penalty or a balloon payment exists. The second section discloses the projected monthly payments over various time periods of the loan. Estimates of the borrower's monthly payment also includes estimated property taxes, insurance, and assessments. This section also shows whether an escrow account exists and how much the borrower should expect to pay each month. The last section on page one provides the estimated amount needed to close.

The second page of the Tupelo prototype uses the example of a loan for $211,000 with $6,151 in closing costs for the sake of illustrating a completed form. The prototype has five sections. The first two sections itemize the various expenses associated with closing.[33] The third section calculates the cash needed to close by summing the settlement fees, settlement costs, down payment, and other costs. Next, a table provides the potential borrower with information on the monthly payments, such as whether there are any interest-only payments and what the maximum payment could be. Finally, a second table describes whether the mortgage interest rate is adjustable and how it could potentially change.

The third page of the Tupelo prototype contains three additional sections. The first section allows borrowers to compare the terms of other loans offered by other loan originators.[34] The section lists the amount that a borrower will have paid in total over the first five years of the loan and how much would go to paying down principal. It also lists the APR as well as the total amount of interest paid over the loan term as a percentage of the loan. The next section provides brief information about other aspects (e.g., appraisal, homeowner's insurance, late payments, and servicing). Should the borrower decide to proceed with the mortgage origination process, the final section provides a space for the applicant to sign to confirm that the form was received.

The CFPB has also developed a prototype settlement disclosure,[35] which consolidates the HUD-1 Settlement Statement and the final TILA disclosure.[36]

## End Notes

[1] The primary rulemaking and enforcement authority of many existing consumer protection laws was transferred to the CFPB by the Dodd-Frank Act. See CRS Report R41338, *The Dodd-Frank Wall Street Reform and Consumer Protection Act: Title X, The Consumer Financial Protection Bureau*, by David H. Carpenter.

[2] TILA is contained in Title I of the Consumer Credit Protection Act, P.L. 90-301, 81 Stat. 146, as amended by 15 U.S.C. Section 1601 et seq.

[3] P.L. 93-533, 88 Stat. 1724, 12 U.S.C. Sections 2601-2617.

[4] The primary rulemaking and enforcement authority of many existing consumer protection laws was transferred to the CFPB by the Dodd-Frank Act. See CRS Report R41338, *The Dodd-Frank Wall Street Reform and Consumer Protection Act: Title X, The Consumer Financial Protection Bureau*, by David H. Carpenter.

[5] The GFE never discusses loan details using the APR term, which is only required on the TILA Disclosure Statement.

[6] For more on the CFPB, see CRS Report R41338, *The Dodd-Frank Wall Street Reform and Consumer Protection Act: Title X, The Consumer Financial Protection Bureau*, by David H. Carpenter.

[7] Bureau of Consumer Financial Protection, "Identification of Enforceable Rules and Orders," 76 *Federal Register* 43569, July 21, 2011.

[8] P.L. 111-203, Section 1098, 12 U.S.C Section 2603.

[9] However, Dodd-Frank states that the bureau does not have to produce a proposed rule if "the Bureau determines that any proposal issued by the Board of Governors and the Secretary of Housing and Urban Development carries out the same purpose." See P.L. 111-203, Section 1032(f).

[10] See Bureau of Consumer Financial Protection, "Know Before You Owe," at http://www .consumerfinance.gov/ knowbeforeyouowe/.

[11] One purpose of simplified disclosure forms is to facilitate consumers' comparison shopping for loan terms. For more information on the extent to which consumers shop to obtain the best mortgage terms, see CRS Report RL 34442, *HUD Proposes Administrative Modifications to the Real Estate Settlement Procedures Act*, by Darryl E. Getter.

[12] P.L. 96-221, 94 Stat. 170, 15 U.S.C. 1604.

[13] Department of Housing and Urban Development, "Real Estate Settlement Procedures Act (RESPA): Rule To Simplify and Improve the Process of Obtaining Mortgages and Reduce Consumer Settlement Costs," 73 *Federal Register* 68204, November 17, 2008.

[14] Department of Housing and Urban Development, "Good Faith Estimate (GFE)," at http://portal.hud.gov/hudportal/ documents/huddoc?id=gfestimate.pdf.

[15] HUD tested the GFE form among various consumer groups; details about these tests may be found at http://www.hud.gov/offices/hsg/sfh/res/200803/summary.pdf.

[16] Department of Housing and Urban Development, "Real Estate Settlement Procedures Act (RESPA): Proposed Rule To Simplify and Improve the Process of Obtaining Mortgages and Reduce Consumer Settlement Costs," 73 *Federal Register* 14035, March 14, 2008.

[17] Federal Reserve System, "Truth In Lending," 74 *Federal Register* 43232, August 26, 2009.

[18] See Patricia A. McCoy, "Rethinking Disclosure in a World of Risk-Based Pricing," *Harvard Journal on Legislation*, vol. 44, no. 1, winter 2007.

[19] James M. Lacko and Janis K. Pappalardo, *Improving Consumer Mortgage Disclosures: An Empirical Assessment of Current and Prototype Disclosure Forms*, Bureau of Economics Staff Report, Federal Trade Commission, June 2007, at http://www.ftc.gov/os/2007/06/P025505MortgageDisclosureReport.pdf.

[20] The APR is the annual cost of a loan, which includes the interest cost of the principal loan amount, insurance, and other fees expressed as a percentage. The mortgage interest rate only includes the interest cost of the principal loan amount expressed as a percentage.

[21] High interest rates and fees may be characteristic of predatory lending but not all loans with high interest rates and fees are predatory. Some borrowers with poor credit histories may have to accept high rates if they wish to borrow from any lender. For more on the complications of defining predatory lending, see James H. Carr and Lopa Kolluri, *Predatory Lending: An Overview*, Fannie Mae Foundation, 2001.

[22] The mortgage interest rate and the YSP are not identical. The YSP is defined as the difference between the total coupon interest rate and the actual wholesale interest rate of the loan. For example, a loan with a market or wholesale rate of 6% may have a total coupon rate of 6.5%, and 0.5% is the compensation going to the mortgage broker, which is the YSP. Some mortgage lenders may pay brokers up to 2% in YSP.

[23] On page two of the revised standardized GFE form, the total origination costs are disclosed in item 1. The division of these costs into points and YSP is disclosed in item 2. A "credit" that represents the dollar value of loan origination costs *not paid at settlement* appears in item 2. In this context, "credit" does not mean the borrower

would receive a refund from the loan originator. Instead, credit refers to the loan origination costs that the borrower still pays, not up front at settlement, but in the form of a higher interest rate, or the YSP. Conversely, the dollar value of fees paid up front at settlement appears as a "charge" in item 2. For a given interest rate, both credit and charge amounts in item 2 should add up to the total loan origination costs, which appears in item 1. The adjusted origination costs, which appear in box A, are the difference between the total loan origination costs and the YSP; the adjusted origination costs refers to the amount of total upfront fees that will be paid at settlement.

24 HUD's testing concluded that 90% of the consumers understood how the trade-off table worked and stated that it was the most useful aspect of the GFE. See Department of Housing and Urban Development, *RESPA: Regulatory Impact Analysis and Initial Regulatory Flexibility Analysis*, FR-5180 5180-F-02, p. 176, at http://www.hud.gov/offices/hsg/ ramh/res/impactanalysis.pdf.

25 HUD estimates that if the GFE added 10 minutes per application, then annual national costs would increase by $255 million if there are 1.7 applications per loan or by $405 million if there are 2.7 applications per loan. Calculations used a $150,000 annual salary and a 2,080 hour work year to determine the hourly wage, which was then scaled to the actual time needed to fill out the forms. See Department of Housing and Urban Development, *RESPA: Regulatory Impact Analysis and Initial Regulatory Flexibility Analysis*, FR-5180 5180-F-02, at http://www.hud.gov/offices/hsg/ramh/res/impactanalysis.pdf.

26 Participants in the HUD study expressed suspicion when the trade-off table was not filled in completely. See http://www.hud.gov/offices/hsg/ramh/res/impactanalysis.pdf, p. 190. In 2009, the state of New Hampshire mandated that the entire trade-off table be completed whenever a yield spread premium is to be collected. If a corresponding loan (with lower settlement charges and a higher interest rate or a lower interest rate and higher settlement charges) is unavailable, the lender fills in "N/A." See New Hampshire Banking Department, "Newsletter," at http://www.nh.gov/banking/NewsletterIssue09_2.pdf.

27 P.L. 104-208, the Economic Growth and Regulatory Paperwork Reduction Act of 1996, directed HUD and the Federal Reserve Board to propose a single form that satisfied the requirements of RESPA and TILA. The Federal Reserve Board and HUD concluded that regulatory changes would not be sufficient and that further statutory changes would be required for the forms to be consolidated. The Dodd-Frank Act provided the necessary legislative authority. See Federal Reserve System, "Truth in Lending," 63 *Federal Register* 6112, February 6, 1998.

28 However, Dodd-Frank states that the bureau does not have to produce a proposed rule if "the Bureau determines that any proposal issued by the Board of Governors and the Secretary of Housing and Urban Development carries out the same purpose." See P.L. 111-203, Section 1032(f).

29 See Consumer Financial Protection Bureau, "Know Before You Owe," at http://www.consumerfinance.gov/knowbefore-you-owe-designing-a-new-disclosure/.

[30] See Consumer Financial Protection Bureau, "SBREFA, Small Providers, and Mortgage Disclosure," at http://www.consumerfinance.gov/blog/sbrefa-small-providers-and-mortgage-disclosure/.

[31] On May 18, 2011, the first two prototypes were made available on the CFPB's website. The Ficus form may be found at http://www.consumerfinance.gov/wp-content/uploads/2011/05/disclosure1.pdf; the Pecan form may be found at http://www.consumerfinance.gov/wp-content/uploads/2011/05/disclosure2.pdf. Other prototypes are also available on the CFPB website. The CFPB website does not provide detailed information on the substance of the comments they have received about the prototypes, nor does it provide an explanation as to why different versions of the prototypes have been altered.

[32] The three page Tupelo document combines the two page TILA Disclosure Statement and three page HUD GFE.

[33] HUD's original GFE lists whether fees can change, can change only by a certain amount, or cannot change between the time they are listed on the GFE and closing. The Tupelo prototype lists what services a borrower can or cannot shop for but does not list tolerances to show how much some fees can increase before closing as is done on the current GFE.

[34] Unlike the GFE, the Tupelo prototype does not include a trade-off table.

[35] See Consumer Financial Protection Bureau, "Know Before You Owe: The last dance... or is it?" at http://www.consumerfinance.gov/blog/know-before-you-owe-the-last-dance-or-is-it/.

[36] The HUD-1 Settlement Statement is the form borrowers receive at the closing that lists all final settlement charges. The HUD-1 Settlement Statement was revised by HUD to be compatible with the numbers provided on its GFE form so that making the comparisons would be easier for borrowers.

In: The Consumer Financial Protection Bureau ISBN 978-1-62257-637-1
Editors: P. J. Cerutti and M. Kolchak 

*Chapter 3*

# THE EARLY AGENDA OF THE CONSUMER FINANCIAL PROTECTION BUREAU: THE NONBANK SUPERVISION PROGRAM*

***Sean M. Hoskins***

## SUMMARY

The Consumer Financial Protection Bureau (CFPB) was established by Title X of the Dodd-Frank Wall Street Reform and Consumer Financial Protection Act (P.L. 111-203, the Dodd-Frank Act). The creation of the CFPB consolidates many existing consumer financial protection responsibilities into one agency.

The Dodd-Frank Act states that the purpose of the CFPB is to implement and enforce federal consumer financial law while ensuring that consumers can access financial products and services. The CFPB is also instructed to ensure that the markets for consumer financial services and products are fair, transparent, and competitive. To fulfill its mandate, the CFPB can issue rules, examine certain institutions, and enforce consumer protection laws and regulations.

On January 4, 2012, President Obama installed Richard Cordray as the director of the Consumer Financial Protection Bureau via recess appointment. The CFPB could not exercise its new powers until a director was appointed.

---

* This is an edited, reformatted and augmented version of Congressional Research Service, Publication No. R42156, dated January 30, 2012.

Included in the newly established powers is the authority to regulate certain nonbanks for consumer protection. Under the new authority conferred by the appointment of Cordray, the CFPB announced the Nonbank Supervision Program. A nonbank is an institution that provides financial services but does not have a bank, thrift, or credit union charter.

The Nonbank Supervision Program will subject some nonbanks to the same consumer protection standards as currently applied to banks. Under the program, the CFPB will supervise three groups of nonbanks.

First, the CFPB can regulate nonbanks in three specific markets—mortgage companies, payday lenders, and private education lenders.

Second, the CFPB can regulate the "larger participants" in other financial markets.

Third, the CFPB may supervise a nonbank that is performing actions that may pose a risk to consumers with regard to consumer financial products or services. This report describes the Nonbank Supervision Program as well as other initiatives that the CFPB has started since its creation.

This report does not address arguments that have been made against the validity of the recess appointment itself, nor does it address related questions that have been raised regarding the scope of Cordray's authority as the director of the CFPB while serving pursuant to a recess appointment.

# INTRODUCTION

One of the first actions by the Consumer Financial Protection Bureau (CFPB) after the appointment of Richard Cordary as its director was to announce its new Nonbank Supervision Program.

A nonbank is an institution that provides financial services or products but does not have a bank, thrift, or credit union charter.[1]

The Nonbank Supervision Program will subject some nonbanks to the same consumer protection standards as currently applied to banks. This report will describe the Nonbank Supervision Program, the structure and powers of the CFPB, and other early CFPB initiatives.

This report does not address arguments that have been made against the validity of the recess appointment itself, nor does it address related questions that have been raised regarding the scope of Cordray's authority as the director of the CFPB while serving pursuant to a recess appointment.[2]

# OVERVIEW OF THE BUREAU

The Consumer Financial Protection Bureau was established by Title X of the Dodd-Frank Wall Street Reform and Consumer Financial Protection Act (P.L. 111-203, the Dodd-Frank Act).[3] The creation of the CFPB consolidates many consumer financial protection responsibilities into one agency. The Dodd-Frank Act states that the purpose of the CFPB is to implement and enforce federal consumer financial law while ensuring that consumers can access financial products and services.[4] The CFPB is also instructed to ensure that the markets for consumer financial services and products are fair, transparent, and competitive.[5] To fulfill its mandate, the CFPB can issue rules, examine certain institutions, and enforce consumer protection laws and regulations.

The Dodd-Frank Act further established that the CFPB is to be headed by a director, appointed by the President by and with the advice and consent of the Senate, who shall serve a five-year term. The bureau is located within the Federal Reserve System (FRS). The Federal Reserve Board, however, cannot veto a rule issued by the CFPB, but the Financial Stability Oversight Council (FSOC), with the vote of two-thirds of its members, can set aside a CFPB proposed rule.[6] The CFPB is funded through the earnings of the FRS, which is not subject to congressional appropriation. The Dodd-Frank Act caps the CFPB's funding at 11% of the FRS's operating expense for FY2011 and at 12% thereafter. If the director determines that additional funding is needed, the Dodd-Frank Act provides authorization for an additional $200 million in appropriations per year through FY2014.

The CFPB has the authority to enforce many of the financial consumer laws,[7] primarily for large depository institutions with assets of more than $10 billion as well as some nonbank institutions.[8] However, some consumer protection responsibilities were not given to the Bureau. The CFPB is not the primary consumer protection regulator of depositories with less than $10 billion in assets. The prudential regulators that regulate the smaller institutions for safety and soundness will continue to regulate them for consumer protection.[9] The Dodd-Frank Act also provides some industries with exemptions from CFPB regulation. The CFPB will not oversee automobile dealers, merchants, retailers, and sellers of nonfinancial goods and services, real estate brokers, real estate agents, sellers of manufactured and mobile homes, income tax preparers, insurance companies, and accountants.[10]

## INITIATIVES UNDERTAKEN BEFORE THE DIRECTOR'S APPOINTMENT

The CFPB has undertaken several policy initiatives since its creation, including the following:[11]

- The "Know Before You Owe" project is simplifying and consolidating disclosure forms for mortgages, credit cards, and student loans.[12] For example, the adequate disclosure of mortgage terms is a long-standing issue that has prompted several congressional actions. The Truth-In-Lending Act (TILA) of 1968[13] and the Real Estate Settlement Procedures Act (RESPA) of 1974[14] were enacted to require disclosures of credit costs and terms to borrowers. The regulatory agencies needed additional legislative action to include both TILA and RESPA disclosures on a single form. The Dodd-Frank Act mandated that the CFPB revisit disclosure stipulations for mortgage loans and gave it the authority to consolidate the mandatory TILA and RESPA disclosures into one "good faith estimate" form.[15]
- The CFPB is collecting mortgage and credit card complaints made by borrowers.[16] CFPB forwards the complaint to the relevant company and keeps the borrower updated on the status of the complaint. Also, the complaints will be used to inform CFPB's supervision of companies and its enforcement of consumer protection laws and regulations.
- The CFPB is providing resources to help servicemembers, veterans, and older Americans handle their unique financial circumstances.[17] For example, the CFPB's Office of Servicemember Affairs is designed to help servicemembers with future financial planning and protecting their personal finances.
- The CFPB will implement rules such as the qualified mortgages rule. On April 19, 2011, the Federal Reserve, as mandated by the Dodd-Frank Act, announced a proposed rule that would require all creditors or lenders to make a good faith estimate that a borrower has a reasonable ability to repay. The rule would also establish minimum mortgage underwriting standards.[18] The rule would expand ability-to-repay standards to cover all residential mortgage loans. The Dodd-Frank Act transferred the authority to prescribe final regulations to the

CFPB on July 21, 2011. CFPB final rulemaking would not necessarily be bound by the Federal Reserve's proposed regulation.[19]

## EARLY AGENDA OF THE NEW DIRECTOR: NONBANK SUPERVISION PROGRAM

On January 4, 2012, President Obama installed Richard Cordray as the director of the Consumer Financial Protection Bureau via recess appointment.[20] As stated in CRS Report R41839, *Limitations on the Secretary of the Treasury's Authority to Exercise the Powers of the Bureau of Consumer Financial Protection*, by David H. Carpenter,

> Until a CFPB Director is appointed, the CFP Act provides the Secretary (of the Treasury) the authority to exercise *some, but not all* of the Bureau's authorities. Although not beyond debate, the CFP Act appears to provide the Secretary the authority to exercise the Bureau's *transferred* powers, but not the authority to exercise the Bureau's *newly established* powers.[21]

The report goes on to state that,

> The Bureau's newly established authorities largely consist of: enhanced, up-front supervisory powers over covered non-depository financial institutions; new rulemaking powers, distinct from the rulemaking authorities provided under the 18 enumerated consumer laws; and certain limited consumer compliance enforcement and examination powers over "smaller depository institutions" (i.e., banks, thrifts, savings associations, and credit unions with $10 billion or less in assets).[22]

Using its "newly established" powers after Cordray's appointment, the CFPB announced its Nonbank Supervision Program. The Nonbank Supervision Program will subject some nonbanks to the same consumer protection standards as currently applied to banks. Under the Program, the CFPB has authority to supervise three groups of nonbanks. First, the CFPB can regulate nonbanks in three specific markets—mortgage companies, payday lenders, and private education lenders. Second, the CFPB can regulate the "larger participants" in other financial markets. Third, the CFPB may supervise a nonbank that is performing actions that may pose a risk to consumers with regard to consumer financial products or services. These three areas of the Nonbank Supervision Program are discussed below.

## Specific Markets

### *Mortgage Companies*

Mortgages are not necessarily originated or serviced just by banks but also by nonbanks. Prior to the financial crisis, nonbanks were a major source of subprime lending, which some point to as one of the possible causes of the financial crisis.[23] The CFPB has authority to oversee nonbank originators, mortgage servicers, and loan modification and foreclosure relief service providers. According to the CFPB, it will investigate allegations of abuse and discrimination directed towards mortgage originators[24] to ensure that they follow applicable laws for consumer protection.[25] In addition, the CFPB will have authority to protect consumers from abuses by bank and nonbank mortgage servicers. Mortgage servicers collect payments from borrowers and forward them to the mortgage holders. If a borrower is delinquent, the servicer facilitates a loss mitigation option to make the loan current or proceeds with a foreclosure. In April 2010, the Federal Reserve, the Office of the Comptroller of the Currency, and the Office of Thrift Supervision issued enforcement actions against some of the largest mortgage servicers because of deficient servicing practices.[26] Servicers were also alleged to have engaged in "robo-signing," where a small number of individuals sign a large number of affidavits and other legal documents that mortgage companies submit to courts and other public authorities to execute foreclosures.[27] The CFPB will attempt to protect consumers from abuses by mortgage servicers through data analysis, onsite examinations, and other forms of monitoring.[28]

### *Payday Lenders*

Under the Nonbank Supervision Program, the CFPB has authority to oversee payday lenders to ensure they comply with federal consumer financial laws. A payday loan is typically a small ($100-$500) cash advance to a borrower who writes a post-dated check for the loan amount plus a fee to the lender, who holds it for a short period of time (until the customer's next payday or 7 to 30 days).[29] Payday lenders require identification, proof of income, and ownership of a checking account, but they do not check into a borrower's credit history or assess the ability to repay the loan. Hence, payday loans are expensive. The fee or financing charge is the equivalent of paying an estimated annual percentage rate (APR) lending rate ranging from 260% to 520%. Such costs for credit may become very expensive for borrowers if they need to be rolled over or extended for additional periods.

Payday loans are considered abusive by some consumer advocates who argue that the industry targets vulnerable consumers. This type of lending may encourage chronic borrowing that causes frequent users to become trapped in a cycle of expensive debt.[30] On the other hand, it is difficult for traditional financial institutions to meet such immediate credit needs if full underwriting costs should exceed the actual loan amounts.[31] In addition, some research has found payday loan fees may even be lower than fees associated with bounced checks or credit card late fees and interest charges.[32]

Although payday loans are still subject to the disclosure provisions of the federal Truth-InLending Act, state laws have generally governed payday lending. State laws, however, are not uniform in their treatment of payday lending. Some states do not have specific payday lending legislation, whereas other states impose limits on finance charges and set a maximum loan amount. Hence, the CFPB has the authority to establish regulations that would achieve consistent lending standards throughout the nation.[33]

### *Private Education Lenders*

The CFPB can regulate nonbank private education lenders under the Nonbank Supervision Program.[34] Private education loans are loans that are used for higher education but are not originated through the federal student loan program.[35] The number of students borrowing and the amount they borrow has been increasing over time.[36] This raises concerns about the burdens of indebtedness as well as the potential for abuse. The CFPB may focus on issues related to the marketing of private education loans to students as well as the disclosures required for these loans. For example, the CFPB is working with the Department of Education to develop a "financial aid shopping sheet" to inform borrowers about their loan options.[37] Also, the Dodd-Frank Act requires the CFPB to partner with the Department of Education and other agencies to publish a report on private education loans and private educational lenders. In November 2011, the CFPB published a request for information about the private education loan market.[38]

### *Defining Larger Participants*

The CFPB has authority to oversee all nonbanks in the residential mortgage, payday lending, and private education lending markets, but can only oversee the nonbank "larger participants" in other financial markets.[39] In June

2011, the CFPB submitted a notice and request for comment on a proposed rule with two main components: determining the threshold that will designate a market participant as "larger" and deciding what markets will be regulated.[40] In determining the threshold, the CFPB solicited comments on, among other things, whether to use absolute or relative measures of size as well as the type of data that should be used. For which markets to regulate, the CFPB proposed six possible industries to monitor: debt collection, consumer reporting, consumer credit, money transmitting and check cashing, prepaid cards, and debt relief services. The CFPB received comments on the proposed rule but has not published the initial rule. The Dodd-Frank Act instructs the CFPB to issue its initial rule on larger participants by July 2012.

## Other Nonbanks

The Dodd-Frank Act gives CFPB authority to supervise a nonbank that would not meet the previously described requirements if, based on the complaints it has received or from other sources, it has reason to believe the nonbank poses risks to consumers in offering its financial services or products.[41] The CFPB has not yet published a final rule to establish procedures to supervise a nonbank under this authority.

## End Notes

[1] See http://www.consumerfinance.gov/the-cfpb-launches-its-nonbank-supervision-program/.

[2] See CRS Report R42323, *President Obama's January 4, 2012, Recess Appointments: Legal Issues*, by David H. Carpenter et al.

[3] See CRS Report R41338, *The Dodd-Frank Wall Street Reform and Consumer Protection Act: Title X, The Consumer Financial Protection Bureau*, by David H. Carpenter.

[4] Dodd-Frank Act §1021.

[5] Ibid.

[6] The FSOC is a council of financial regulators, including CFPB, that is charged with monitoring systemic risk in the financial system and coordinating several federal financial regulators. For more on the FSOC, see CRS Report R42083, *Financial Stability Oversight Council: A Framework to Mitigate Systemic Risk*, by Edward V. Murphy. The authority to review CFPB regulations is found in Dodd-Frank §1023.

[7] For the list of the enumerated consumer laws that have been transferred to the CFPB see Dodd-Frank Section 1002.

[8] For more on the CFPB's authority over nonbanks, see the section 'Early Agenda of the New Director: Nonbank Supervision Program' in this report.

[9] For more on the regulation of financial institutions, see CRS Report R40249, *Who Regulates Whom? An Overview of U.S. Financial Supervision*, by Mark Jickling and Edward V. Murphy.

[10] The Dodd-Frank Act provides exceptions such that, under certain conditions, the CFPB may regulate these otherwise excluded industries. See CRS Report R41338, *The Dodd-Frank Wall Street Reform and Consumer Protection Act: Title X, The Consumer Financial Protection Bureau*, by David H. Carpenter.

[11] This section does not provide a comprehensive list of CFPB initiatives but highlights some of it current efforts.

[12] See http://www.consumerfinance.gov/knowbeforeyouowe/.

[13] TILA is contained in Title I of the Consumer Credit Protection Act, P.L. 90-301, 81 Stat. 146, as amended by 15 U.S.C. Section 1601 et seq.

[14] P.L. 93-533, 88 Stat. 1724, 12 U.S.C. Sections 2601-2617.

[15] For a more through discussion of the progress CFBP has made with respect to implementing RESPA, see CRS Report R41980, *Revisiting Mortgage Loan Disclosures Under the Consumer Financial Protection Bureau*, by Darryl E. Getter and Sean M. Hoskins.

[16] See https://help.consumerfinance.gov/app/mortgage/ask and https://help.consumerfinance.gov/app/ ask_cc_complaint.

[17] See http://www.consumerfinance.gov/servicemembers/ and http://www.consumerfinance.gov/older-americans/.

[18] See http://www.federalreserve.gov/newsevents/press/bcreg/20110419a.htm. The rule was published in the *Federal Register* on May 11, 2011. See http://www.gpo.gov/fdsys/pkg/FR-2011-05-11/pdf/2011-9766.pdf. General rulemaking authority for the Truth-in-Lending Act, which is implemented under Regulation Z, transfers to the CFPB on July 21, 2011. See CRS Report R41338, *The Dodd-Frank Wall Street Reform and Consumer Protection Act: Title X, The Consumer Financial Protection Bureau*, by David H. Carpenter. For more information about the proposed rule, see CRS Report R42056, *Ability to Repay, Risk-Retention Standards, and Mortgage Credit Access*, by Darryl E. Getter.

[19] See CRS Report R41839, *Limitations on the Secretary of the Treasury's Authority to Exercise the Powers of the Bureau of Consumer Financial Protection*, by David H. Carpenter.

[20] As noted above this report does not address questions that have been raised regarding the validity or effect of this recess appointment. For more on recess appointments, see CRS Report RS21308, *Recess Appointments: Frequently Asked Questions*, by Henry B. Hogue, and CRS Report RL33009, *Recess Appointments: A Legal Overview*, by Vivian S. Chu.

[21] See CRS Report R41839, *Limitations on the Secretary of the Treasury's Authority to Exercise the Powers of the Bureau of Consumer Financial Protection*, by David H. Carpenter.

[22] See CRS Report R41839, *Limitations on the Secretary of the Treasury's Authority to Exercise the Powers of the Bureau of Consumer Financial Protection*, by David H. Carpenter.

[23] See CRS Report R40173, *Causes of the Financial Crisis*, by Mark Jickling.

[24] For an example of allegations of discrimination by a mortgage originator, see the Department of Justice's settlement with Bank of America. United States Department of Justice, "Justice Department Reaches $335 Million Settlement to Resolve Allegations of Lending Discrimination by Countrywide Financial Corporation," press release, December 21, 2011, http://www.justice.gov/opa/pr/2011/December/11-ag-1694.html.

[25] See http://www.consumerfinance.gov/pressrelease/consumer-financial-protection-bureau-releases-mortgageorigination-examination-procedures/.

[26] See http://www.occ.gov/news-issuances/news-releases/2011/nr-occ-2011-47a.pdf.

[27] See CRS Report R41491, *"Robo-Signing" and Other Alleged Documentation Problems in Judicial and Nonjudicial Foreclosure Processes*, by David H. Carpenter.

[28] See http://www.consumerfinance.gov/pressrelease/consumer-financial-protection-bureau-releases-mortgageorigination-examination-procedures/.

[29] See CRS Report RS21728, Payday Loans: Federal Regulatory Initiatives, by Pauline Smale and Determinants of the Locations of Payday Lenders, Pawnshops, and Check-Cashing Outlets by Robin A. Prager, Board of Governors of the Federal Reserve System, Finance and Economics Discussion Series 2009-33, Washington, DC, June 2009, http://www.federalreserve.gov/pubs/feds/2009/200933/200933pap.pdf.

[30] See Center for Responsible Lending, *Payday Loans Put Families in the Red*, CRL Issue Brief, February 2009, http://www.responsiblelending.org/payday-lending/research-analysis /payday-puts-families-in-the-red-final.pdf.

[31] See Edward C. Lawrence and Gregory Elliehausen, "A Comparative Analysis of Payday Loan Customers," *Contemporary Economic Policy*, April 2008, pp. 299-316.

[32] See Donald P. Morgan and Michael R. Strain, *Payday Holiday: How Households Fare After Payday Credit Bans*, Federal Reserve Bank of New York, Staff Reports no. 309, New York, NY, February 2008, http://www.newyorkfed.org/research/staff_reports/sr309.pdf.

[33] The CFPB held a field hearing on payday lending products on January 19, 2012, in Birmingham, Alabama. See http://www.consumerfinance.gov/pressrelease/consumer-financial-protection-bureau-convenes-field-hearing-inbirmingham-alabama-on-payday-lending/.

[34] For more on private education lenders, see CRS Report RL34654, *The Higher Education Opportunity Act: Reauthorization of the Higher Education Act*, by David P. Smole et al.

[35] See http://www.consumerfinance.gov/pressrelease/consumer-financial-protection-bureau-aims-to-shed-light-on-theprivate-student-loan-industry/.

[36] For example, more than $100 billion in student loans were taken out in 2010, which increases the outstanding education debt total to more than $1 trillion. See http://www.usatoday. com/ money/perfi/college/story/2011-10-19/student-loan-debt/50818676/1. Also, approximately $7.9 billion of student loans in 2010 came from private and state sources, but these sectors had provided $24 billion in student loans in 2007. See http://trends. collegeboard.org/ downloads/Student_Aid_2011.pdf.

[37] See http://www.consumerfinance.gov/students/knowbeforeyouowe/.

[38] See Consumer Financial Protection Bureau, "Request for Information Regarding Private Education Loans and Private Educational Lenders," 76 *Federal Register* 71329-71331, November 17, 2011.

[39] Dodd-Frank §1024 (a)(1)(B).

[40] Consumer Financial Protection Bureau, "Defining Larger Participants in Certain Consumer Financial Products and Services Markets," 76 *Federal Register* 38059-38062, August 15, 2011.

[41] Dodd-Frank §1024 (a)(1)(C). As mentioned previously, see CRS Report R41338, *The Dodd-Frank Wall Street Reform and Consumer Protection Act: Title X, The Consumer Financial Protection Bureau*, by David H. Carpenter, for when previously exempted industries may be regulated by the CFPB.

In: The Consumer Financial Protection Bureau ISBN 978-1-62257-637-1
Editors: P. J. Cerutti and M. Kolchak 

*Chapter 4*

# THE DODD-FRANK WALL STREET REFORM AND CONSUMER PROTECTION ACT: REGULATIONS TO BE ISSUED BY THE CONSUMER FINANCIAL PROTECTION BUREAU*

***Curtis W. Copeland***

## SUMMARY

Title X of the Dodd-Frank Wall Street Reform and Consumer Protection Act (P.L. 111-203, July 21, 2010) consolidates many federal consumer protection responsibilities into a new Bureau of Consumer Financial Protection (often referred to as the Consumer Financial Protection Bureau, or CFPB) within the Federal Reserve System. The act transfers supervisory and enforcement authority over a number of consumer financial products and services to the Bureau on a still-to-be-determined transfer date during calendar year 2011. Title X and Title XIV of the act contain numerous provisions that require or permit the CFPB to issue regulations implementing the statute's provisions. This report describes those provisions, notes that certain regulatory oversight tools

---

* This is an edited, reformatted and augmented version of Congressional Research Services publication R41380, dated August 25, 2010.

will not be available for CFPB rules, and discusses the authority of a council of bank regulators to "set aside" the Bureau's rules.

Section 1022 alone gives the CFPB broad rulemaking powers, authorizing it to prescribe such rules "as may be necessary or appropriate" to enable the Bureau to administer federal consumer financial protection laws. The act contains many other provisions that require or permit the Bureau to issue rules, most of which give the Bureau substantial discretion regarding whether rules need to be issued, the contents of those rules, and when they must be issued. The Bureau also assumes responsibility for certain transferor agencies' existing rules, proposed rules that have not been made final, and final rules that have not taken effect. Therefore, other than for about 20 rules that are specifically required in the statute, it is not currently possible to determine how many rules the Bureau will issue, or the contents of those rules. Although most of the Bureau's rulemaking authority and discretion is the same as it was before being transferred from the safety and soundness (prudential) regulators, it is not clear that those authorities and discretion will be exercised in the same way.

Like other independent regulatory agencies, some regulatory oversight methods will not be available for CFPB rules. The Bureau's significant rules will not be reviewed by the Office of Management and Budget (OMB) under Executive Order 12866, and those rules will not be subject to the cost-benefit analysis requirements in the order. The Bureau may be able to void OMB disapprovals of its collections of information under the Paperwork Reduction Act. Because the CFPB might not receive appropriated funds, Congress may not be able to control the Bureau's rulemaking through appropriations restrictions. Also, the effectiveness of new requirements placed on the Bureau to examine its rules within five years, and to take certain actions under the Regulatory Flexibility Act, may depend on how the Bureau interprets key terms.

Congress did, however, empower the newly created Financial Stability Oversight Council (composed primarily of the heads of the prudential regulatory agencies from which the CFPB was formed) to "stay" or "set aside" all or part of a Bureau rule that it concludes would put the safety and soundness of the U.S. banking or financial systems at risk. No other executive branch entity (including OMB) has previously been given the authority to nullify an agency's rules, and the authority to set aside a portion of a rule is greater than the expedited authority Congress gave itself through the Congressional Review Act (CRA). However, several aspects of the Council review process are currently unclear (e.g., whether the Council must vote to stay a rule).

Although Congress may not be able to use appropriations restrictions to control CFPB rulemaking, Congress still has an array of oversight tools available, including confirmation hearings, oversight hearings, meetings between individual Members and the Bureau, and CRA resolutions of disapproval.

# INTRODUCTION

The Dodd-Frank Wall Street Reform and Consumer Protection Act (P.L. 111-203, July 21, 2010, hereafter, the "Dodd-Frank Act") was enacted in the wake of what many believe was the worst U.S. financial crisis since the Great Depression. The legislation addresses a variety of issues that arose as a result of that crisis, one of which was the perception that the federal system of consumer protection was fragmented and, in some cases, inconsistent with other regulatory functions.[1] For example, safety and soundness (prudential) regulators and consumer protection regulators may look on the same activity differently. Therefore, some argued that separating prudential and consumer protection regulation into separate agencies is the best way to protect both consumers and financial institutions.

Until the Dodd-Frank Act fully goes into effect, the Board of Governors of the Federal Reserve System will continue to write rules to implement most of the consumer financial protection laws. Enforcement of these laws is shared by a variety of prudential regulators, including the Office of the Comptroller of the Currency for national banks; the Federal Reserve Board for domestic operations of foreign banks and for state-chartered banks that are members of the Federal Reserve System; the Federal Deposit Insurance Corporation for state-chartered banks and other state-chartered banking institutions that are not members of the Federal Reserve System; the National Credit Union Administration for federally insured credit unions; and the Office of Thrift Supervision for federal savings and loan associations and thrifts. The Federal Trade Commission is the primary federal regulator for non-depository financial institutions (e.g., payday lenders and mortgage brokers) and many other non-financial commercial enterprises.[2]

## Consumer Financial Protection Bureau

Title X of the Dodd-Frank Act, entitled the "Consumer Financial Protection Act of 2010,"[3] consolidates many federal consumer protection responsibilities into a new Bureau of Consumer Financial Protection (often referred to as the Consumer Financial Protection Bureau, CFPB, or Bureau) within the Federal Reserve System.[4] The act gives the CFPB rulemaking, enforcement, and supervisory authority over a variety of consumer financial products and services (and many of the entities that offer these products and services), and transfers to the Bureau rulemaking and enforcement authority over many previously enacted consumer protection laws. The Bureau's authority varies according to the type of company,[5] and the act explicitly exempts certain entities and activities from the Bureau's authority.[6]

Congress created the CFPB as an independent regulatory agency within the Federal Reserve System (which is, itself, an independent regulatory agency).[7] Such agencies are intended to be more independent of the President than cabinet departments and other executive branch agencies.[8] The Bureau is to be headed by a director, who is appointed by the President, with the advice and consent of the Senate, to a five-year term of office. The director can only be removed from office for "inefficiency, neglect of duty, or malfeasance in office."[9] Until a director is confirmed, the Secretary of the Treasury assumes all of the powers of the director. The CFPB is funded, up to certain caps, using proceeds from the combined earnings of the Federal Reserve System, which the Dodd-Frank Act says are not reviewable by either the House or the Senate appropriations committees.[10] Using the Federal Reserve System's operating expenses as a baseline, the CFBP could receive up to about $550 million for FY2011. However, if the director of the CFPB determines that these funds are insufficient, the act authorizes appropriations of up to $200 million per year for FY2010 through FY2014.

Some portions of the Consumer Financial Protection Act went into effect on the date of enactment, while many other parts of the act go into effect on the "designated transfer date," which the Secretary of the Treasury is required to establish not later than 60 days after the date of enactment (i.e., by September 19, 2010).[11] The act generally requires that the transfer date "be not earlier than 180 days, nor later than 12 months, after the date of enactment of this Act" (i.e., between January 17, 2011, and July 21, 2011).[12] Between the date of enactment and that transfer date, the Board of Governors of the Federal Reserve System ("Board of Governors") is required to transfer to the Bureau "the amount estimated by the Secretary needed to carry out the authorities granted to the Bureau under Federal consumer financial law."[13]

Section 1063(i) of the Dodd-Frank Act requires the Bureau, no later than the designated transfer date, to consult with the head of each agency transferring consumer protection functions and "identify the rules and orders that will be enforced by the Bureau." The agreed-upon list of rules and orders must be published in the *Federal Register*. Section 1063(j) states that "Any proposed rule of a transferor agency which that agency, in performing consumer financial protection functions transferred by this title, has proposed before the designated transfer date, but has not been published as a final rule before that date, shall be deemed to be a proposed rule of the Bureau." It also says that "any interim or final rule of a transferor agency which that agency, in performing consumer financial protection functions transferred by this title, has published before the designated transfer date, but which has not become effective before that date, shall become effective as a rule of the Bureau according to its terms."[14]

## This Report

In addition to the above-mentioned general provisions making the CFPB responsible for transferor agencies' existing and pending rules, Title X of the Dodd-Frank Act contains numerous specific provisions that require or permit the Bureau to issue new regulations implementing the act's provisions. Title XIV of the act, entitled the "Mortgage Reform and Anti-Predatory Lending Act,"[15] also contains several provisions that require or permit the Bureau to issue rules. Commenters on the Dodd-Frank Act have expressed both concerns and hopes regarding the effects that these and other financial reform rules will have on the economy and on consumer protection,[16] with the operation of the CFPB a particular concern to some observers. [17] By one count, the legislation mentions a total of 243 "rulemakings" that are expected to occur pursuant to the act, with the Bureau accounting for 24 of those actions.[18] Others have placed the number of rules expected to be issued pursuant to the act even higher.[19]

This report describes the rulemaking provisions in Titles X and XIV of the Dodd-Frank Act that pertain to the CFPB.[20] To identify those provisions, CRS searched through the text of Titles X and XIV in the enrolled version of H.R. 4173 as passed by the House of Representatives and the Senate (because the text of the public law was not yet available) using certain words and terms ("regulation," "final rule," "proposed rule," "rulemaking," "prescribe rules," "prescribe regulations," "by rule," and "such rules"). The results of that effort are provided in a table in the **Appendix** to this report. Although this process identified more than 50 CFPB-related rulemaking provisions, it is unclear whether the searches identified all such provisions in the legislation. (For example, other rulemaking provisions may have used other terms.) The report also notes that while some regulatory oversight procedures and requirements will not apply to CFPB rules, the Dodd-Frank Act gives a council composed primarily of prudential regulators substantial authority to dispose of the Bureau's rules.

The table in the **Appendix** is organized into two groups: (1) provisions that require the CFPB to issue regulations (e.g., stating that the Bureau "shall prescribe regulations..."); and (2) provisions that permit, but do not require, the issuance of regulations (e.g., stating that the CFPB "may prescribe rules..."). For each such provision, the table provides the section number in the Dodd-Frank Act, the relevant text of the provision, whether the act requires the participation of other agencies in the development or issuance of the rule, and any deadlines delineated in the act regarding the issuance or implementation of the rules.

### *Provisions Not Included in the Table*

The table in the **Appendix** does not include some general regulatory provisions in Titles X and XIV, including certain wholesale transfers of rulemaking authority from one agency to the CFPB. For example, Section 1061(b)(5)(A) states that the "authority of the Federal Trade Commission under an enumerated consumer law to prescribe rules, issue guidelines, or conduct a study or issue a report mandated under such law shall be transferred to the Bureau on the designated transfer date." While it is possible that the Bureau may issue regulations pursuant to these types of transferred authorities, cataloguing all of the rulemaking authorities covered by this provision is beyond the scope of this report. Also, as noted previously, the CFPB and the prudential regulators have until the designated transfer date to decide which existing rules the Bureau will enforce.

The table also does not include provisions in the Dodd-Frank Act that may result in regulations, but that do not specifically require or permit rulemaking. For example, Section 1463(a) of the act amended Section 6 of the Real Estate Settlement Procedures Act of 1974 (12 U.S.C. 2605), and states (in part) that

> A servicer of a federally related mortgage shall accept any reasonable form of written confirmation from a borrower of existing insurance coverage, which shall include the existing insurance policy number along with the identity of, and contact information for, the insurance company or agent, or as otherwise required by the Bureau of Consumer Financial Protection.

Pursuant to this provision, the Bureau may issue regulations establishing written confirmation requirements. However, because the legislation did not specifically require or permit the issuance of rules, this provision is not included in the table.

Finally, the table does not include any rulemaking authorities involving the internal operation of the Bureau. For example, Section 1012(a)(1) of the Dodd-Frank Act authorizes the Bureau to establish general policies with respect to all executive and administrative functions, including "the establishment of rules for conducting the general business of the Bureau." This provision is not included in the table.

## CFPB, Like Transferor Agencies, Has Broad Rulemaking Authority

In addition to the previously mentioned provisions in Section 1063 of the Dodd-Frank Act making the CFPB generally responsible for transferor agencies' existing and pending rules, Titles X and XIV of the act contain more than 50 provisions that transfer certain rulemaking authorities to the CFPB, or that give the Bureau new rulemaking authority. These provisions sometimes require the Bureau to issue certain rules, but they more often give the agencies the discretion to decide whether to issue rules within a particular area, and if so, what those rules will contain. Although most of the Bureau's legal rulemaking authority and discretion is the same as it was before being transferred from the prudential regulators, it is not clear that those authorities and discretion will be exercised in the same way.

### Section 1022 and CFPB Rulemaking

Section 1022 of the act alone ("Rulemaking Authority") gives the CFPB broad rulemaking powers and responsibilities. For example, Section 1022(a) states that the Bureau is "authorized to exercise its authorities under Federal consumer financial law to administer, enforce, and otherwise implement the provisions of Federal consumer financial law." Section 1022(b)(1) permits the director of the Bureau to "prescribe rules and issue orders and guidance, as may be necessary or appropriate to enable the Bureau to administer and carry out the purposes and objectives of the Federal consumer financial laws, and to prevent evasions thereof."

The term "Federal consumer financial laws" is defined as including the new authorities provided in Title X, the authorities that were transferred to the Bureau under subtitles F and H, and the authorities in certain "enumerated consumer laws,"[21] which generally include[22]

- the Alternative Mortgage Transaction Parity Act of 1982 (12 U.S.C. 3801 et seq.);
- the Consumer Leasing Act of 1976 (15 U.S.C. 1667 et seq.);
- the Electronic Fund Transfer Act (15 U.S.C. 1693 et seq.), except with respect to section 920 of that act;
- the Equal Credit Opportunity Act (15 U.S.C. 1691 et seq.);
- the Fair Credit Billing Act (15 U.S.C. 1666 et seq.);
- the Fair Credit Reporting Act (15 U.S.C. 1681 et seq.), except with respect to sections 615(e) and 628 of that act (15 U.S.C. 1681m(e), 1681w);
- the Home Owners Protection Act of 1998 (12 U.S.C. 4901 et seq.);
- the Fair Debt Collection Practices Act (15 U.S.C. 1692 et seq.);
- subsections (b) through (f) of section 43 of the Federal Deposit Insurance Act (12 U.S.C. 1831t(c)-(f));
- Sections 502 through 509 of the Gramm-Leach-Bliley Act (15 U.S.C. 6802- 6809) except for section 505 as it applies to section 501(b);
- the Home Mortgage Disclosure Act of 1975 (12 U.S.C. 2801 et seq.);
- the Home Ownership and Equity Protection Act of 1994 (15 U.S.C. 1601 note);
- the Real Estate Settlement Procedures Act of 1974 (12 U.S.C. 2601 et seq.);
- the S.A.F.E. Mortgage Licensing Act of 2008 (12 U.S.C. 5101 et seq.);
- the Truth in Lending Act (15 U.S.C. 1601 et seq.);
- the Truth in Savings Act (12 U.S.C. 4301 et seq.);
- Section 626 of the Omnibus Appropriations Act, 2009 (P.L. 111-8); and
- the Interstate Land Sales Full Disclosure Act (15 U.S.C. 1701).

As discussed in detail in the next section of this report, the CFPB's rulemaking activities are subject to all of the applicable government-wide requirements (e.g., the Administrative Procedure Act), as well as the specific requirement in the enumerated consumer laws being transferred to the Bureau.

In addition, Section 1022(b)(2) of the Dodd-Frank Act says that, in prescribing a rule under the federal consumer financial laws, the Bureau must "consider...the potential benefits and costs to consumers and covered persons," "the impact of proposed rules on covered persons," and "the impact on consumers in rural areas."[23] It also requires the Bureau to "consult with the appropriate prudential regulators or other Federal agencies prior to proposing a rule and during the comment process regarding (the rule's) consistency with prudential, market, or systemic objectives administered by such agencies." If a prudential regulator provides the CFPB with a written objection to all or part of a proposed rule, the Bureau is required to "include in the adopting release a description of the objection and the basis for the Bureau decision, if any, regarding such objection."[24] Notably, however, while these federal regulators and agencies can file objections to the Bureau's draft rules, Section 1022 does not permit them to prevent the rules from going forward.

Also, Section 1022(b)(4) states that, with one exception,[25]

> to the extent that a provision of Federal consumer financial law authorizes the Bureau and another Federal agency to issue regulations under that provision of law for purposes of assuring compliance with Federal consumer financial law and any regulations thereunder, the Bureau shall have the exclusive authority to prescribe rules subject to those provisions of law.

It also says that "the deference that a court affords to the Bureau with respect to a determination by the Bureau regarding the meaning or interpretation of any provision of a Federal consumer financial law shall be applied as if the Bureau were the only agency authorized to apply, enforce, interpret, or administer the provisions of such Federal consumer financial law."[26]

***Related Authorities and Duties***

To support its rulemaking functions, the CFPB is required to "monitor for risks to consumers in the offering or provision of consumer financial products or services."[27] As part of this monitoring effort, the Bureau is authorized to

> require covered persons and service providers participating in consumer financial services markets to file with the Bureau, under oath or otherwise, in such form and within such reasonable period of time as the Bureau may prescribe by rule or order, annual or special reports, or answers in writing to specific questions.[28]

To determine whether a nondepository institution (e.g., a payday lender or a mortgage broker) is a “covered person,” the CFPB is authorized to require the nondepository “to file with the Bureau, under oath or otherwise, in such form and within such reasonable period of time as the Bureau may prescribe by rule or order, annual or special reports, or answers in writing to specific questions.”[29] In addition, Section 1022(c)(7) of the act permits the CFPB to prescribe rules regarding registration requirements applicable to “covered persons” (other than an insured depository institution, insured credit union, or related person). The section also permits the Bureau to issue rules regarding the disclosure of that registration information to the public.[30]

The Bureau is required to publish at least one report per year regarding the “significant findings of its monitoring,” with the first report required “beginning with the first calendar year that begins at least 1 year after the designated transfer date.”[31] However, the Bureau is also allowed to make public, through reports or “other appropriate formats,” any other information that it obtains from its monitoring effort that it determines is “in the public interest,” provided that any confidential information that it collects is protected.[32] To the extent that the Bureau’s rulemaking is an outgrowth of such monitoring, the interested public may be able to review those reports and determine what CFPB rules could be forthcoming.[33]

***Rule Effectiveness Reports***

Section 1022(d) of the act requires the CFPB to publish a report assessing the effectiveness of each “significant rule or order” within five years of it taking effect.[34] The act requires these assessments to address, among other things, “the effectiveness of the rule or order in meeting the purposes and objectives of this title and the specific goals stated by the Bureau.” Before publishing the required report, the CFPB is required to obtain comments from the public about any recommendations for modifying, expanding, or eliminating the significant rule or order.

## Other Rulemaking Requirements and Authorities

In addition to the broad rulemaking powers provided by Section 1022, Titles X and XIV of the Dodd-Frank Act also contain dozens of other provisions that require or permit the CFPB to issue regulations. Most of those provisions give the Bureau substantial discretion regarding whether, and if so, how rules should be crafted. Some sections are more specific, and describe what the rules should contain and/or how they should be promulgated. Most of the provisions in Title X authorize only the Bureau to issue rules, whereas almost all of the provisions in Title XIV require the rules to be issued jointly with a group of other agencies. Also, while a few of the rulemaking provisions in Title X indicate when the rules must be issued or implemented, in most cases the title is silent regarding the timing of the rules. Title XIV, on the other hand, contains a general provision stipulating when rules issued under the title must be published and take effect.

### *Most Provisions Provide Bureau Discretion*

The non-mandatory rulemaking provisions in the Dodd-Frank Act arguably provide the CFPB with the greatest amount of discretion, allowing the Bureau to decide whether any regulations will be developed at all, and if issued, what the rules will contain. For example:

- Section 1071(a) of the act (amending the Equal Credit Opportunity Act (15 U.S.C. 1691 et seq.)) states that the Bureau "shall prescribe such rules and issue such guidance as may be necessary to carry out, enforce, and compile data pursuant to this section (on small business data collection)." Therefore, the Bureau can decide whether regulations or guidance in this area are "necessary," and if so, what any such rules will require.
- Section 1097(1) (amending Section 626 of the Omnibus Appropriations Act, 2009 (15 U.S.C. 1638 note)) says the Bureau "shall have authority to prescribe rules with respect to mortgage loans in accordance with section 553 of title 5, United States Code. Such rulemaking shall relate to unfair or deceptive acts or practices regarding mortgage loans, which may include unfair or deceptive acts or practices involving loan modification and foreclosure rescue services." [35] The Bureau can decide whether or not to use this rulemaking authority, and (within the parameters provided in this section) can determine the content of any rules that it decides to issue.

Although the mandatory provisions in the act require that certain rules be issued, they often give the Bureau substantial discretion regarding how the required rules will be crafted. For example:

- Section 1022(c)(6)(A) states that the Bureau "shall prescribe rules regarding the confidential treatment of information obtained from persons in connection with the exercise of its authorities under Federal consumer financial law." This provision does not prescribe either the content of the required rules or how they should be developed.

- Section 1024(b)(7)(A) requires the Bureau to "prescribe rules to facilitate supervision of persons described in subsection (a)(1) and assessment and detection of risks to consumers." Section 1024 relates to "Supervision of Nondepository Covered Persons," and subsection (a)(1) states that the section applies to any covered person who, among other things, "offers or provides origination, brokerage, or servicing of loans secured by real estate for use by consumers primarily for personal, family, or household purposes, or loan modification or foreclosure relief services in connection with such loans;" or "offers or provides to a consumer a payday loan." The section does not indicate how the required rules should be crafted or what they should contain.
- Section 1042(c) requires the Bureau to "prescribe regulations to implement the requirements of this section" (on "Preservation of Enforcement Powers of the States"). Although Section 1042 prescribes certain legal authorities and consultation requirements, the section does not otherwise indicate what the required regulations must contain.
- Section 1053(e) states that the Bureau "shall prescribe rules establishing such procedures as may be necessary to carry out this section" (on "Hearings and Adjudication Proceedings"). Section 1053 delineates special rules for cease-anddesist proceedings and enforcement of orders, but does not otherwise prescribe the contents of those rules.
- Section 1100(6)(B) states that the Bureau "is authorized to promulgate regulations setting minimum net worth or surety bond requirements for residential mortgage loan originators and minimum requirements for recovery funds paid into by loan originators." In issuing those regulations, the section requires the Bureau to "take into account the need to provide originators adequate incentives to originate affordable and sustainable mortgage loans, as well as the need to ensure a competitive origination market that maximizes consumer access to affordable and sustainable mortgage loans." Otherwise, the section does not indicate what those rules should contain.

As was the case with the discretionary provisions, some of the mandatory rulemaking provisions in Title X and Title XIV of the Dodd-Frank Act amend other statutes, and give the CFPB broad transferred authority within those amended statutes. For example, Section 1084 of the act amends the Electronic Fund Transfer Act (15 U.S.C. 1693 et seq.) and states that, with certain exceptions, the Bureau "shall prescribe rules to carry out the purposes of this title." (This section transferred certain rulemaking authorities from the Board of Governors of the Federal Reserve System to the CFPB.)

Certain sections of the act appear to allow the Bureau to take other, non-rulemaking actions to satisfy the underlying requirement. For example, Section 1002(25) states that the definition of a "related person" includes "any shareholder, consultant, joint venture partner, or other person, as determined by the Bureau (by rule or on a case-by-case basis) who materially participates in the conduct of the affairs of such covered person." Therefore, the Bureau could issue a rule defining these terms, or could adjudicate each case individually. Also, Section 1079(c) of the act requires the Bureau to "propose regulations or otherwise establish a program to protect consumers who use exchange facilitators." Therefore, the Bureau could issue a rule to protect consumers, or could do so by establishing a program.

***Some Provisions Prescribe Rule Contents or Process***

In contrast to the previously mentioned broad grants of rulemaking authority, some CFPB-related rulemaking provisions in Titles X and XIV, or the statutes amended by those titles, prescribe the contents of the rules that the statute requires or permits the Bureau to issue. For example, Section 1473(f)(2) of the act requires the Bureau and other agencies to "jointly, by rule, establish minimum requirements to be applied by a State in the registration of appraisal management companies." That provision also states the following:

> Such requirements shall include a requirement that such companies—(1) register with and be subject to supervision by a State appraiser certifying and licensing agency in each State in which such company operates; (2) verify that only licensed or certified appraisers are used for federally related transactions; (3) require that appraisals coordinated by an appraisal management company comply with the Uniform Standards of Professional Appraisal Practice; and (4) require that appraisals are conducted independently and free from inappropriate influence and coercion pursuant to the appraisal independence standards established under section 129E of the Truth in Lending Act.

Section 1094(3)(B) of the act (amending the Home Mortgage Disclosure Act of 1975 (12 U.S.C. 2801 et seq.)) also specifies the content of the required rule. That section requires the Bureau to

> develop regulations that (A) prescribe the format for such disclosures, the method for submission of the data to the appropriate agency, and the procedures for disclosing the information to the public; (B) require the collection of data required to be disclosed under subsection (b) with respect to loans sold by each institution reporting under this title; (C) require disclosure of the class of the purchaser of such loans; (D) permit any reporting institution to submit in writing to the Bureau or to the appropriate agency such additional data or explanations as it deems relevant to the decision to originate or purchase mortgage loans; and (E) modify or require modification of itemized information, for the purpose of protecting the privacy interests of the mortgage applicants or mortgagors, that is or will be available to the public.

Some of the rulemaking authorities transferred to the Bureau also contain specific requirements. For example, Section 1088(a)(9) of the act amended the Fair Credit Reporting Act (15 U.S.C. 1681 et seq.) and states that the Bureau "shall prescribe rules to carry out this subsection." (Previously, this rulemaking authority had been jointly provided to the Federal Trade Commission and the Board of Governors.) As had been the case with regard to the agencies who were previously required to issue these rules, the Bureau's rules are required to address

> (i) the form, content, time, and manner of delivery of any notice under this subsection; (ii) clarification of the meaning of terms used in this subsection, including what credit terms are material, and when credit terms are materially less favorable; (iii) exceptions to the notice requirement under this subsection for classes of persons or transactions regarding which the agencies determine that notice would not significantly benefit consumers; (iv) a model notice that may be used to comply with this subsection; and (v) the timing of the notice required under paragraph (1), including the circumstances under which the notice must be provided after the terms offered to the consumer were set based on information from a consumer report.[36]

**Procedural Requirements**

Some provisions in Titles X and XIV specify the process by which CFPB rules should be developed or issued. For example, Section 1041(c)(1) of the act requires the Bureau to "issue a notice of proposed rulemaking whenever a majority of states has enacted a resolution in support of the establishment or modification of a consumer protection regulation by the Bureau." The next paragraph states that

> Before prescribing a final regulation based upon a notice issued pursuant to paragraph (1), the Bureau shall take into account whether (A) the proposed regulation would afford greater protection to consumers than any existing regulation; (B) the intended benefits of the proposed regulation for consumers would outweigh any increased costs or inconveniences for consumers, and would not discriminate unfairly against any category or class of consumers; and (C) a Federal banking agency has advised that the proposed regulation is likely to present an unacceptable safety and soundness risk to insured depository institutions.

The section goes on to require the Bureau to include a discussion of these considerations in the *Federal Register* notice of any final regulation. If the Bureau decides not to issue a final regulation, the statute requires it to "publish an explanation of such determination in the Federal Register, and provide a copy of such explanation to each State that enacted a resolution in support of the proposed regulation, the Committee on Banking, Housing, and Urban Affairs of the Senate, and the Committee on Financial Services of the House of Representatives."[37]

Other provisions also establish certain procedural requirements for rulemaking. For example:

- Section 1024(a)(2) states that the Bureau "shall consult with the Federal Trade Commission prior to issuing a rule...to define covered persons subject to this section" (on "Supervision of Nondepository Covered Persons").
- Section 1094 requires the Bureau to issue certain rules "in consultation with other appropriate agencies."

As noted previously in this report, although these and other provisions require the CFPB to consult with other agencies before issuing their rules, the act does not permit those agencies to prevent the issuance of the rules.

Most of the provisions in Title X require or permit the CFPB alone to issue the required or permitted rules. Exceptions include (1) Section 1025(e)(4)(E), which requires the Bureau to prescribe certain rules with the "prudential regulators;" and (2) Section 1088(b)(3), which requires the Bureau, the Commodity Futures Trading Commission, and the Securities and

Exchange Commission to each issue regulations carrying out Section 624 of the Fair Credit Reporting Act. In contrast, the provisions in Title XIV of the act almost always require that the Bureau issue the required rules jointly with the Board of Governors, the Comptroller of the Currency, the Federal Deposit Insurance Corporation, the National Credit Union Administration Board, and the Federal Housing Finance Agency.[38]

### *Publication and Effective Dates*

Most of the individual provisions in Titles X and XIV of the Dodd-Frank Act that require or permit CFPB to issue rules do not specify when those rules must be published or take effect. To the extent that the timing of the rules is mentioned in those provisions, the issuance is always keyed to the designated transfer date. For example:

- Section 1024(a)(2) states that the "initial rule" must be issued within one year of the transfer date.
- Section 1079(c) requires that a proposed rule be issued (or a program be established) within two years after the submission of a report, which is required within one year of the transfer date.
- Section 1083(a) of the act (amending the Alternative Mortgage Transaction Parity Act of 1982 (12 U.S.C. 3801 et seq.)) requires that regulations be promulgated "after the designated transfer date."

In contrast to the timing discretion given to the Bureau in Title X, Section 1400(c) of the legislation states that all of the regulations required under Title XIV must "(A) be prescribed in final form before the end of the 18-month period beginning on the designated transfer date; and (B) take effect not later than 12 months after the date of issuance of the regulations in final form." It goes on to say that sections or provisions in that title "shall take effect on the date on which the final regulations implementing such section, or provision, take effect." Sections for which regulations have not been issued are required to take effect 18 months after the designated transfer date.

## Rulemaking Authority and Discretion Generally the Same

Although the Dodd-Frank Act gives the CFPB some new responsibilities, most of its rulemaking authority and discretion was transferred to the Bureau through the enumerated consumer laws. With regard to those laws, the Bureau has the same amount of rulemaking authority and discretion as the prudential regulators that previously were responsible for them. What is different, however, is that the consumer protection powers provided by those laws are now vested in a single agency, and that agency now has as its primary mission to "regulate the offering and provision of consumer financial products or services."[39] Whether those contextual differences will result in different regulations, or different application of existing rules, is currently unclear.

## SOME FEDERAL RULEMAKING REQUIREMENTS NOT APPLICABLE TO CFPB RULES

During the past 65 years, Congress and various presidents have developed an elaborate set of procedures and requirements to guide and oversee the federal rulemaking process. Statutory requirements include the Administrative Procedure Act, the Regulatory Flexibility Act, the Paperwork Reduction Act, the Unfunded Mandates Reform Act, and the Congressional Review Act—each of which requires that certain procedural and/or analytical requirements be addressed before agencies' rules can be published and take effect.[40] The scope and effectiveness of these and other congressional efforts to control the rulemaking process vary. For example, although Congress has used the Congressional Review Act (5 U.S.C. 801-808) to disapprove only one final rule in more than 14 years,[41] every year Congress adds a number of provisions to agencies' appropriations bills stating that "none of the funds" provided through the legislation can be used to initiate rulemaking in certain areas, to make certain proposed rules final, or to implement certain final rules.[42]

Presidential review of agency rulemaking is currently centered in Executive Order 12866, which requires covered agencies to submit their "significant" regulatory actions to the Office of Information and Regulatory Affairs (OIRA) within the Office of Management (OMB) before they are published in the *Federal Register*.[43] OIRA reviews the rules to determine their consistency with the analytic requirements in the executive order, the statutes under which they are issued, the President's priorities, and the rules issued by other agencies. The executive order requires that the agencies "propose or adopt a regulation only upon a reasoned determination that the benefits of the intended regulation justify its costs."[44] Covered agencies are required to estimate the costs and benefits of their "significant" rules, and to conduct a full cost-benefit analysis before issuing any "economically significant" rule (e.g., one that is expected to have a $100 million annual impact on the economy).[45] That analysis is required to include an assessment of not only the underlying benefits and costs, but also the costs and benefits of "potentially effective and reasonably feasible alternatives to the planned regulation."[46]

OIRA also plays a key role in implementing the requirements of the Paperwork Reduction Act (PRA, 44 U.S.C. 3501-3520). The PRA created OIRA, and generally requires that agencies receive OIRA approval for certain information collection requests before they are conducted. Before approving a proposed collection of information, OIRA must determine whether the collection is "necessary for the proper performance of the functions of the agency."[47] OIRA's information collection approvals must be renewed at least every three years if the agency wishes to continue collecting the information.

## Many Rulemaking Requirements, and Exceptions, Apply to CFPB Rules

Many of the government-wide rulemaking requirements appear to apply to rulemaking by the CFPB, but the exceptions and exemptions to those requirements also apply. For example, the Administrative Procedure Act (APA, 5 U.S.C. 551 *et seq.*) generally requires that federal agencies publish a notice of proposed rulemaking in the *Federal Register*, give "interested persons" an opportunity to comment on the rule, consider those comments and publish a final rule with a general statement of its basis and purpose, and make the final rule effective no less than 30 days after its publication.[48] However, the APA also says that these "notice and comment" procedures do not apply when the agency finds, for "good cause," that those procedures are "impracticable, unnecessary, or contrary to the public interest."[49] Also, agencies can make their rules take effect less than 30 days after they are published if there is "good cause."[50] Therefore, for example, if the CFPB concludes that time constraints or other factors make public comments "impracticable," the agency can publish the final rule without a prior proposed rule or comment period. Agencies' use of the APA's good cause exceptions are subject to judicial review.

Also, the Regulatory Flexibility Act (RFA, 5 U.S.C. 601-612) requires federal agencies to assess the impact of their forthcoming rules on "small entities," which includes small businesses, small governmental jurisdictions, and small not-for-profit organizations.[51] Under the RFA, federal agencies must prepare a regulatory flexibility analysis at the time that proposed and certain final rules are published in the *Federal Register*. The act requires the analyses to describe, among other things, (1) why the regulatory action is being considered and its objectives; (2) the small entities to which the rule will apply and, where feasible, an estimate of their number; (3) the projected reporting, recordkeeping, and other compliance requirements of the rule; and, for final rules, (4) steps the agency has taken to minimize the impact of the rule on small entities. However, these requirements are not triggered if the head of the issuing agency certifies that the rule would not have a "significant economic impact on a substantial number of small entities." The RFA does not define "significant economic impact" or "substantial number of small entities," thereby giving federal agencies substantial discretion regarding when the act's analytical requirements are initiated.[52] Also, the RFA's analytical requirements do not apply when an agency publishes a final rule without publishing a prior proposed rule.[53] Therefore, if the CFPB publishes a final rule using the APA's "good cause" exception, the RFA's analytical requirements do not apply.

## Some Rulemaking Requirements and Controls Are Not Applicable to the CFPB

In addition to these exceptions and exclusions, some notable regulatory oversight mechanisms do not appear to apply to the CFPB's rules at all, or may be able to be voided by the Bureau. These requirements are also not applicable to most, if not all, of the independent regulatory agencies from whom rulemaking authorities were transferred.

### *Executive Order 12866*

For example, most of the requirements in Executive Order 12866 do not apply to independent regulatory agencies like the CFPB.[54] Therefore, the Bureau does not have to submit its proposed or final significant rules to OIRA for review before they are published. Also, CFPB does not have to conduct cost-benefit analyses for its economically significant rules, and does not have to show that the benefits of its significant rules "justify" the costs. Although Sections 1022 and 1041(c)(1) of the Dodd-Frank Act require the Bureau to "consider" and "take into account" the potential benefits and costs of its rules, these provisions appear to establish somewhat lower analytical thresholds than the requirement in Executive Order 12866 that the benefits of agencies' rules "justify" the costs.

### *Paperwork Reduction Act*

Also, although the Paperwork Reduction Act covers independent regulatory agencies like the CFPB, and permits OIRA to disapprove their proposed collections of information, the Bureau may be able to collect the information even if OIRA objects. The PRA states that

> An independent regulatory agency which is administered by 2 or more members of a commission, board, or similar body, may by majority vote void (A) any disapproval by the Director (of OMB), in whole or in part, of a proposed collection of information of that agency; or (B) an exercise of authority under subsection (d) of section 3507 concerning that agency (regarding information collections that are part of a proposed rule).[55]

Although the CFPB is an independent regulatory agency, it is headed by a single director, not a multi-member body. Therefore, this provision would not appear to apply to the Bureau. However, Section 1100D(c) of the Dodd-Frank Act amends the PRA, and states that

> Notwithstanding any other provision of law, the Director (of OMB) shall treat or review a rule or order prescribed or proposed by the Director of the Bureau of Consumer Financial Protection on the same terms and conditions as apply to any rule or order prescribed or proposed by the Board of Governors of the Federal Reserve System.

Applying this subsection, because the Board of Governors, a multi-member board, is authorized to void OIRA disapprovals of its information collections, the director of the CFPB may arguably be authorized to do so as well.

### *Unfunded Mandates Reform Act*

The Unfunded Mandates Reform Act (UMRA) of 1995 was enacted in an effort to reduce the costs associated with federal imposition of responsibilities, duties, and regulations upon state, local, and tribal governments and the private sector without providing the funding appropriate to the costs imposed by those responsibilities. Title II of UMRA (2 U.S.C. 1532-1538) generally requires cabinet departments and other agencies to prepare a written statement containing specific descriptions and estimates for any proposed rule that is expected to result in the expenditure of $100 million or more in any year to state, local, or tribal governments, or to the private sector.

However, UMRA does not apply to independent regulatory agencies, and therefore does not apply to any of the CFPB's rules. Even if UMRA did apply to the CFPB, UMRA contains so many other exceptions and exclusions that its requirements might not apply to most of the agency's rules.[56]

### *Appropriations Restrictions*

Appropriations restrictions may also be unavailable as a way for Congress to control the Bureau's rulemaking. As noted earlier in this report, the CFPB is funded (up to certain caps) using money from the combined earnings of the Federal Reserve System, and the Dodd-Frank Act states that those funds are not reviewable by either the House or the Senate appropriations committees.[57] Therefore, since the Bureau might not receive appropriated funds, Congress may not be able to encourage or restrict rulemaking through the kinds of appropriations restrictions that it has frequently used with regard to other agencies' rules.

## Effectiveness of New Rulemaking Requirements Depends on How the Bureau Interprets Key Terms

The Dodd-Frank Act made three amendments to the Regulatory Flexibility Act, adding requirements that are particular to the CFPB. Also, as noted previously, the Dodd-Frank Act requires the Bureau to examine certain rules within five years of their issuance. The effectiveness of these new rulemaking requirements may depend on how the CFPB interprets certain key terms.

### *Regulatory Flexibility Act Amendments*

As noted previously in this report, the RFA requires all covered federal agencies (including independent regulatory agencies like the CFPB) to conduct a "regulatory flexibility analysis" before publishing any proposed or final rule that is expected to have a "significant economic impact on a substantial number of small entities." Section 1100G(b) of the Dodd-Frank Act adds a Bureau-specific provision to the government-wide requirements for proposed rule analyses, stating that the CFPB must also describe

> (A) any projected increase in the cost of credit for small entities; (B) any significant alternatives to the proposed rule which accomplish the stated objectives of applicable statutes and which minimize any increase in the cost of credit for small entities; and (C) advice and recommendations of

> representatives of small entities relating to issues described in subparagraphs (A) and (B) and (the initial regulatory flexibility analysis).

Also, Section 1100G(c) of the Dodd-Frank Act adds a Bureau-specific requirement to the existing requirements for a final rule analysis, stipulating that the Bureau must include "a description of the steps the agency has taken to minimize any additional cost of credit for small entities."

Since 1996, the RFA has required the Environmental Protection Agency and the Occupational Safety and Health administration to hold "advocacy review panels" before developing proposed rules that are expected to have a "significant economic impact on a substantial number of small entities."[58] Section 1100G(a) of the Dodd-Frank Act amended the RFA and requires the CFPB to hold such panels as well.

However, the CFPB does not have to convene an advocacy review panel or conduct an RFA analysis if it issues a final rule without a prior notice of proposed rulemaking (e.g., by using the APA's "good cause" exception), or if it certifies that the rule is not expected to have a "significant economic impact on a substantial number of small entities." Because the RFA does not define the terms "significant economic impact" or "substantial number of small entities," the CFPB, like other federal agencies, will have a substantial amount of discretion regarding when the act's requirements are triggered.

### *"Lookback" Requirement*

The previously mentioned "lookback" provision in Section 1022(d) of the Dodd-Frank Act requires that the CFPB examine and report on the effectiveness of its "significant' rules and orders within five years of their issuance. However, Section 1022(d) does not define what rules should be considered "significant," and does not indicate how "effectiveness" should be measured. Therefore, the Bureau appears to have considerable discretion in determining which rules will have to be reviewed, and whether they will be considered "effective" or not.

Also, although the Dodd-Frank Act requires the Bureau to allow the public to comment before publishing its report, those comments are only required regarding any recommendations for modifying, expanding, or eliminating a rule or order. Thus, if the Bureau determines that a rule is effective, and therefore decides not to change the rule, the act does not appear to require public comments.

## OVERSIGHT COUNCIL IS PERMITTED TO "STAY" OR "SET ASIDE" CFPB REGULATIONS

Although certain regulatory oversight mechanisms appear to be inapplicable or subject to interpretation by the CFPB, the Dodd-Frank Act establishes a new oversight mechanism that is arguably more powerful than any that had previously existed. Section 1023 of the act ("Review of Bureau Regulations") puts in place a procedure by which a Bureau rule, or a provision thereof, can be stayed or "set aside" by the newly-established Financial Stability Oversight Council if the Council concludes that the regulation or provision would "put the safety and soundness of the United States banking system or the ability of the financial system of the United States at risk."[59]

The Financial Stability Oversight Council was established by Section 111 of the Dodd-Frank Act. Voting members of the Council are (1) the Secretary of the Treasury, who serves as Chairperson of the Council; (2) the Chairman of the Board of Governors; (3) the Comptroller of the Currency; (4) the Director of the Bureau; (5) the Chairman of the Securities and Exchange Commission; (6) the Chairperson of the Federal Deposit Insurance Corporation; (7) the Chairperson of the Commodity Futures Trading Commission; (7) the Director of the Federal Housing Finance Agency; (8) the Chairman of the National Credit Union Administration Board; and (9) "an independent member appointed by the President, by and with the advice and consent of the Senate, having insurance expertise." Nonvoting members are (A) the Director of the Office of Financial Research within the Department of the Treasury;[60] (B) the Director of the Federal Insurance Office within the Department of the Treasury;[61] (C) "a State insurance commissioner, to be designated by a selection process determined by the State insurance commissioners"; (D) "a State banking supervisor, to be designated by a selection process determined by the State banking supervisors"; and (E) "a State securities commissioner (or an officer performing like functions), to be designated by a selection process determined by such State securities commissioners."

Section 1023(b) states that an "agency represented by a member of the Council" may petition the Council in writing to stay the effectiveness or set aside a Bureau regulation.[62] First, however, the agency must have, "in good faith," attempted to work with the Bureau to resolve its concerns regarding the effect of the rule on the banking or financial systems. Also, the petition must have been filed within 10 days after the rule was published in the *Federal*

*Register*, and the petition must be published in the *Federal Register* and transmitted "contemporaneously" to the Senate Committee on Banking, Housing, and Urban Affairs, and to the House Committee on Financial Services.

If any "member agency" of the Council so requests, the Chairperson is permitted to stay the effectiveness of a CFPB rule for up to 90 days to permit the Council to consider the petition.[63] A decision to issue a stay of, or to set aside, a Bureau rule requires an affirmative vote by two-thirds "of the Members of the Council then serving," and must be taken within 45 days following the date the petition is filed, or by the expiration of a stay issued by the Council, whichever is later.[64] A decision by the Council to set aside a rule (or a provision therein) renders it "unenforceable," and the Council must publish that decision and its reasoning in the *Federal Register* "as soon as practicable after the decision."[65] The Council's decision to set aside a rule or a provision thereof is subject to judicial review under Chapter 7 of Title 5, *United States Code*.[66]

## Unique Authority

The authority of the Financial Stability Oversight Council to stay or "set aside" final rules issued by the CFPB is unique. No other agency or organization in the executive branch of the federal government is currently permitted to unilaterally stop or nullify another agency's published final rule. Executive Order 12866 allows OIRA within OMB to return a covered agency's draft rule to the agency for "reconsideration" before it is published, but the executive order does not permit OIRA to simply "set aside" an agency's published final rule.

Also, Section 1023 permits the Council to revoke either an entire final rule or a "provision thereof." In this respect, the Council's authority is greater than the expedited disapproval authority that Congress granted to itself through the Congressional Review Act, which only permits revocation of final rules in their entirety.[67] (Congress could, of course, use its regular legislative authority to disapprove all or part of a CFPB rule.)

The Dodd-Frank Act does not provide any procedure by which the actions of the Council can be checked by the President or Congress. Nevertheless, if Congress and the President wanted a revoked Bureau rule to go into effect, legislation could be enacted that would reverse the Council's decision and/or place the rule in statute. Also, Section 1023(c)(8) of the Dodd-Frank Act subjects a Council revocation to judicial review.

It is notable that the voting members of the Financial Stability Oversight Council are the heads of the agencies from which the CFPB's consumer protection rulemaking and enforcement authorities were drawn. Therefore, these prudential regulatory agencies, relieved of most of their consumer protection functions, will potentially be able to stop the Bureau's consumer protection regulations if they conclude, by a two-thirds vote, that those regulations would put the banking or financial systems "at risk."

There are several aspects of the Council's revocation procedures that are currently unclear. For example:

- Before filing a petition, an agency must have acted "in good faith" to resolve its concerns regarding the effect of the rule on the banking or financial systems. It is unclear who determines whether the agency has, in fact, acted "in good faith," or what types of actions will be considered to meet that standard.
- The act states that the chairperson of the Council is permitted to stay the effectiveness of any rule for up to 90 days, upon a request by a "member agency." However, the statute also says that a decision to stay a rule requires an affirmative vote by two-thirds of the Council. It is unclear whether the chairperson can stay a rule for 90 days without such a vote.
- The act states that the Council can void a CFPB final rule if it concludes that it would put the safety and soundness of the banking or financial systems "at risk," but it is not clear what types of rules would meet that standard.
- Also, as discussed in the final section of this report on "Oversight Options," it is unclear whether the Council's decision to set aside a CFPB rule is, itself, a "rule" that must be submitted to Congress under the Congressional Review Act, and that can be disapproved by Congress using the expedited procedures contained therein.

## CONCLUDING OBSERVATIONS

Although Titles X and XIV of the Dodd-Frank Act contain more than 50 provisions that specifically require or permit the CFPB to issue regulations, the actual number of rules that will be issued by the Bureau pursuant to the act's authority is currently unknowable. For example:

- About 20 sections in the act specifically require that the CFPB issue rules, but the agency may issue multiple rules under a single provision.
- Other sections of the act allow the Bureau to promulgate such rules "as may be necessary" to implement those sections, including the broad rulemaking authority provided in Section 1022(b)(1). Therefore, subject to the consultation and considerations attendant to this provision (as well as the constraints of applicable government-wide rulemaking requirements), the CFPB will arguably be able to issue whatever rules it decides are "necessary or appropriate," even if no other sections of the statute provided specific rulemaking authority. On the other hand, the Bureau may decide to issue no new rules under these types of authorities.
- Still other sections of the Dodd-Frank Act do not mention rulemaking at all, but may be implemented through CFPB rules.[68]
- Section 1063 of the Dodd-Frank Act makes the CFPB responsible for certain rules that have been issued by an agency transferring consumer protection functions to the Bureau, any proposed rule that a transferor agency has not made final as of the designated transfer date, and any final rule issued by a transferor agency that has not taken effect. It is currently unclear how many rules that the Bureau will assume pursuant to these provisions, or how many amendments to those transferred rules that the Bureau will issue in the future.

Because of these and other factors, efforts to determine with precision how many rulemaking provisions are in the statute seem misplaced, for they will not necessarily provide useful clues as to how many or what type of rules the Bureau is likely to issue.

## Congressional Oversight Options

Even though it is impossible to predict with any certainty what rules the CFPB will issue, it is clear that the Bureau has been given significant rulemaking authority. However, several of the mechanisms that have been used for decades to oversee and control rulemaking do not appear to be available with regard to the CFPB. The substance of the Bureau's significant rules will not be reviewed by OIRA under Executive Order 12866, it appears that the Bureau can void OIRA disapprovals of its collections of information under the PRA, and Congress may not be able to require or restrict rulemaking in particular areas through appropriation restrictions (because the Bureau, at least initially, may not receive appropriated funds). Also, the effectiveness of provisions in the Dodd-Frank Act that increased the Bureau's requirements under the RFA, as well as a provision requiring an evaluation of the Bureau's rules within five years of their issuance, appear dependent on how the CFPB interprets those provisions.

Nevertheless, Congress still has a number of oversight tools available to affect the nature of CFPB rulemaking, including

- confirmation hearings for the still-to-be-selected director of the Bureau;
- oversight hearings on the Bureau's implementation of the act; and
- meetings between individual Members and representatives of the Bureau regarding pending rules, and filing comments on the rules.[69]

As one author indicated,

> [I]nvestigations conducted by congressional committees constitute another powerful device of formal political supervision.... The public legislative hearings, in which administrative action is carefully scrutinized and a commissioner or staff member is plied with questions, symbolizes the unparalleled sophistication of American congressional control over administrative action, in general and by [independent regulatory agencies], in particular. Individual oversight by representatives or senators also takes place. Through correspondence or meetings, the latter convey the concerns of their constituents.[70]

### *Congressional Review Act*

Another congressional oversight option regarding the Bureau's rules is the Congressional Review Act, which was enacted in 1996 in an attempt to reestablish a measure of congressional authority over rulemaking "without at the same time requiring Congress to become a super regulatory agency."[71] The act generally requires all federal agencies (including independent regulatory agencies) to submit all of their covered final rules to both houses of Congress and GAO before they can take effect.[72] It also established expedited legislative procedures (primarily in the Senate) by which Congress may disapprove agencies' final rules by enacting a joint resolution of disapproval.[73] The definition of a covered rule in the CRA is quite broad, arguably including any type of document (e.g., legislative rules, policy statements, guidance, manuals, and memoranda) that the agency wishes to make binding on the affected public.[74] After a rule is submitted, Congress can use the expedited procedures specified in the CRA (particularly in the Senate) to disapprove of the rule. CRA resolutions of disapproval must be presented to the President for signature or veto.

For a variety of reasons, however, the CRA has been used to disapprove only one rule in the more than 14 years since it was enacted.[75] Perhaps most notably, it is likely that a President would veto a resolution of disapproval to protect rules developed under his own administration, and it may be difficult for Congress to muster the two-thirds vote in both houses needed to overturn the veto. Congress can also use regular (i.e., non-CRA) legislative procedures to disapprove agencies' rules, but such legislation may prove even more difficult to enact than a CRA resolution of disapproval (primarily because of the lack of expedited procedures in the Senate), and if enacted may also be vetoed by the President. These difficulties notwithstanding, even if the use of the CRA does not result in the disapproval of a rule, just the threat of filing of a resolution of disapproval can sometimes exert pressure on agencies to modify or withdraw their rules.[76]

### Are Council Decisions "Rules" Under the CRA?

Although it is clear that the Bureau's rules are subject to the CRA, it is not clear whether a decision by the Financial Stability Oversight Council to "set aside" a Bureau rule is, itself, a "rule" under the CRA. Section 1023(c)(6) of the Dodd-Frank Act requires the Council's decisions to stay or set aside a rule be published in the *Federal Register*, and Section 1023(c)(7) states that the APA's notice and comment rulemaking procedures (5 U.S.C. 553) "shall not apply" to such decisions. Notably, however, the act does not state that the Council's decisions are not rules under Section 551 of the APA, and says that a Council decision to set aside a Bureau regulation is subject to judicial review (i.e., in the same manner as an agency rule would be). On the other hand, it is not clear that Congress intended the Council's actions to be considered "rules" that could be disapproved using CRA procedures. The Council itself appears to have been delegated no specific rulemaking authority.

# APPENDIX. REGULATIONS TO BE ISSUED BY THE CONSUMER FINANCIAL PROTECTION BUREAU

| Section | Text of the Provision | Other Agencies | Deadlines for Rules |
|---|---|---|---|
| Mandatory Regulations (e.g., "shall prescribe rules … ") | | | |
| Section 1022(c)(6)(A) | "…shall prescribe rules regarding the confidential treatment of information obtained from persons in connection with the exercise of its authorities under Federal consumer financial law." | None | None |
| Section 1024(a)(2) | "…shall consult with the Federal Trade Commission prior to issuing a rule, in accordance with paragraph (1)(B), to define covered persons subject to this section…" (on "Supervision of Nondepository Covered Persons"). | Consultation with the Federal Trade Commission | "Initial rule" required within one year after the designated transfer date. |
| Section 1024(b)(7)(A) | " … shall prescribe rules to facilitate supervision of persons described in subsection (a)(1) and assessment and detection of risks to consumers." | None | None |
| Section 1025(e)(4)(E) | "…shall prescribe rules to provide safeguards from retaliation against the insured depository institution, insured credit union, or other covered person described in subsection (a) instituting an appeal under this paragraph, as well as their officers and employees." | Rules to be issued with the "prudential regulators." | None |

## Appendix. (Continued)

| Section | Text of the Provision | Other Agencies | Deadlines for Rules |
|---|---|---|---|
| Section 1033(d) | "…by rule, shall prescribe standards applicable to covered persons to promote the development and use of standardized formats for information, including through the use of machine readable files, to be made available to consumers under this section" (on "Consumer Rights to Access Information"). | None | None |
| Section 1035(c) | "The Ombudsman designated under this subsection (re private education loans) shall…in accordance with regulations of the Director, receive, review, and attempt to resolve informally complaints from borrowers of loans described in subsection (a), including, as appropriate, attempts to resolve such complaints in collaboration with the Department of Education and with institutions of higher education, lenders, guaranty agencies, loan servicers, and other participants in private education loan programs." | None | None |
| Section 1041(c)(1) | "The Bureau shall issue a notice of proposed rulemaking whenever a majority of the States has enacted a resolution in support of the establishment or modification of a consumer protection regulation by the Bureau." | Impetus for rulemaking is the enactment of resolutions by a majority of the States. | None |
| Section 1042(c) | "…shall prescribe regulations to implement the requirements of this section…" (on "Preservation of Enforcement Powers of the States"). | None | None |

| Section | Text of the Provision | Other Agencies | Deadlines for Rules |
|---|---|---|---|
| Section 1053(e) | "…shall prescribe rules establishing such procedures as may be necessary to carry out this section" (on "Hearings and Adjudication Proceedings"). | None | None |
| Section 1071(a) (amending the Equal Credit Opportunity Act (15 U.S.C. 1691 et seq.)) | "Each financial institution shall compile and maintain, in accordance with regulations of the Bureau, a record of the information provided by any loan applicant pursuant to a request under subsection (b)." | None | None |
| Section 1071(a) (amending the Equal Credit Opportunity Act (15 U.S.C. 1691 et seq.)) | "Information compiled and maintained under this section ("Small Business Loan Data Collection") shall be—(A) retained for not less than 3 years after the date of preparation; (B) made available to any member of the public, upon request, in the form required under regulations prescribed by the Bureau; (C) annually made available to the public generally by the Bureau, in such form and in such manner as is determined by the Bureau, by regulation." | None | None |
| Section 1079(c) | "…shall, consistent with subtitle B ("General Powers of the Bureau"), propose regulations or otherwise establish a program to protect consumers who use exchange facilitators." | None | Rule or program must be established within two years after the submission of a report (which is required within one year of the transfer date). |

## Appendix. (Continued)

| Section | Text of the Provision | Other Agencies | Deadlines for Rules |
|---|---|---|---|
| Section 1083(a) (amending the Alternative Mortgage Transaction Parity Act of 1982 (12 U.S.C. 3801 et seq.)) | Bureau is required to determine whether the existing regulations applicable under paragraphs (1) through (3) of subsection (a) are "fair and not deceptive and otherwise meet the objectives of the Consumer Financial Protection Act of 2010," and "(3) promulgate regulations under subsection (a)(4)…." | None | Regulations to be promulgated "after the designated transfer date." |
| Section 1084 (amending the Electronic Fund Transfer Act (15 U.S.C. 1693 et seq.) | " ... shall prescribe rules to carry out the purposes of this title" (with certain exceptions). | None | None |
| Section 1088(a)(9) (amending the Fair Credit Reporting Act (15 U.S.C. 1681 et seq.) | "…shall prescribe rules to carry out this subsection" (on amendments to the Fair Credit Reporting Act). | None | None |
| Section 1088(a)(11)(C) (amending the Fair Credit Reporting Act (15 U.S.C. 1681 et seq.)) | "…shall, with respect to persons or entities that are subject to the enforcement authority of the Bureau under section 621…prescribe regulations requiring each person that furnishes information to a consumer reporting agency to establish reasonable policies and procedures for implementing the guidelines established pursuant to subparagraph (A)." | None | None |

| Section | Text of the Provision | Other Agencies | Deadlines for Rules |
|---|---|---|---|
| Section 1088(b)(3) | "Regulations to carry out section 624 of the Fair Credit Reporting Act (15 U.S.C. 1681s-3), shall be prescribed, as described in paragraph (2), by…." | Rules to be issued by (1) the Commodity Futures Trading Commission, with respect to entities subject to its enforcement authorities; (2) the Securities and Exchange Commission, with respect to entities subject to its enforcement authorities; (3) the Bureau, with respect to other entities subject to this legislation. | None |
| Section 1094(3)(B) (amending the Home Mortgage Disclosure Act of 1975 (12 U.S.C. 2801 et seq.)) | "…, shall develop regulations that (A) prescribe the format for such disclosures, the method for submission of the data to the appropriate agency, and the procedures for disclosing the information to the public; (B) require the collection of data required to be disclosed under subsection (b) with respect to loans sold by each institution reporting under this title; (C) require disclosure of the class of the purchaser of such loans; (D) permit any reporting institution to submit in writing to the Bureau or to the appropriate agency such additional data or explanations as it deems relevant to the decision to originate or purchase mortgage loans; and (E) modify or require modification of itemized information, for the purpose of protecting the privacy interests of the mortgage applicants or mortgagors, that is or will be available to the public." | Rule to be developed in consultation with "appropriate banking agencies," the Federal Deposit Insurance Corporation, the National Credit Union Administration Board, and the Secretary of Housing and Urban Development. | None |

## Appendix. (Continued)

| Section | Text of the Provision | Other Agencies | Deadlines for Rules |
|---|---|---|---|
| Section 1094(3)(F) (amending the Home Mortgage Disclosure Act of 1975 (12 U.S.C. 2801 et seq.)) | "The data required to be disclosed under subsection (b) shall be submitted to the Bureau or to the appropriate agency for any institution reporting under this title, in accordance with regulations prescribed by the Bureau." | None | None |
| Section 1463(a) (amending Section 6 of the Real Estate Settlement Procedures Act of 1974 (12 U.S.C. 2605)) | "A servicer of a federally related mortgage shall not…charge fees for responding to valid qualified written requests (as defined in regulations which the Bureau of Consumer Financial Protection shall prescribe) under this section" (or) "fail to comply with any other obligation found by the Bureau of Consumer Financial Protection, by regulation, to be appropriate to carry out the consumer protection purposes of this Act." | None | Per Section 1400(c), final rule to be published within 18 months after designated transfer date, and to take effect within 12 months after issuance. |
| Section 1471 (amending Chapter 2 of the Truth in Lending Act (15 U.S.C. 1631 et seq.)) | "…shall jointly prescribe regulations to implement this section" ("Property Appraisal Requirements"). It goes on to say that the agencies "may jointly exempt, by rule, a class of loans from the requirements of this subsection or subsection (a) if the agencies determine that the exemption is in the public interest and promotes the safety and soundness of creditors." | Rule to be issued jointly with the Board of Governors, Comptroller of the Currency, Federal Deposit Insurance Corporation, National Credit Union Administration Board, and the Federal Housing Finance Agency | Per Section 1400(c), final rule to be published within 18 months after designated transfer date, and to take effect within 12 months after issuance. |

| Section | Text of the Provision | Other Agencies | Deadlines for Rules |
|---|---|---|---|
| Section 1473(f)(2) (amending Title XI of the Financial Institutions Reform, Recovery, and Enforcement Act of 1989 (12 U.S.C. 3331 et seq.)) | "…shall jointly, by rule, establish minimum requirements to be applied by a State in the registration of appraisal management companies." | Rule to be issued jointly with the Board of Governors, the Comptroller of the Currency, the Federal Deposit Insurance Corporation, the National Credit Union Administration Board, and the Federal Housing Finance Agency | Per Section 1400(c), final rule to be published within 18 months after designated transfer date, and to take effect within 12 months after issuance. |
| Section 1473(f)(2) (amending Title XI of the Financial Institutions Reform, Recovery, and Enforcement Act of 1989 (12 U.S.C. 3331 et seq.)) | "…shall jointly promulgate regulations for the reporting of the activities of appraisal management companies to the Appraisal Subcommittee in determining the payment of the annual registry fee." | Rule to be issued jointly with the Board of Governors of the Federal Reserve System, the Comptroller of the Currency, the Federal Deposit Insurance Corporation, the National Credit Union Administration Board, and the Federal Housing Finance Agency | Per Section 1400(c), final rule to be published within 18 months after designated transfer date, and to take effect within 12 months after issuance. |
| Section 1473(q) (amending Title XI of the Financial Institutions Reform, Recovery, and Enforcement Act of 1989 (12 U.S.C. 3331 et seq.)) | "…shall promulgate regulations to implement the quality control standards required under this section" (on automated valuation models used to estimate collateral value for mortgage lending purposes). | Rule to be issued jointly with the Board of Governors, the Comptroller of the Currency, the Federal Deposit Insurance Corporation, the National Credit Union Administration Board, and the Federal Housing Finance Agency, in consultation with the staff of the Appraisal Subcommittee and the Appraisal Standards Board of the Appraisal Foundation | Per Section 1400(c), final rule to be published within 18 months after designated transfer date, and to take effect within 12 months after issuance. |

## Appendix. (Continued)

| Section | Text of the Provision | Other Agencies | Deadlines for Rules |
|---|---|---|---|
| Discretionary Regulations (e.g., "may prescribe rules…") | | | |
| Section 1002(9) | The term "deposit-taking activity" includes "the receipt of funds or the equivalent thereof, as the Bureau may determine by rule or order, received or held by a covered person (or an agent for a covered person) for the purpose of facilitating a payment or transferring funds or value of funds between a consumer and a third party." | None | None |
| Section 1002(15)(A) | The definition of the term "financial product or service" includes "…such other financial product or service as may be defined by the Bureau, by regulation, for purposes of this title, if the Bureau finds that such financial product or service is—(I) entered into or conducted as a subterfuge or with a purpose to evade any Federal consumer financial law; or (II) permissible for a bank or for a financial holding company to offer or to provide under any provision of a Federal law or regulation applicable to a bank or a financial holding company, and has, or likely will have, a material impact on consumers." | None | None |

| Section | Text of the Provision | Other Agencies | Deadlines for Rules |
| --- | --- | --- | --- |
| Section 1002(25) | The definition of a "related person" includes "any shareholder, consultant, joint venture partner, or other person, as determined by the Bureau (by rule or on a case-by-case basis) who materially participates in the conduct of the affairs of such covered person." | None | None |
| Section 1022(b)(1) | "…may prescribe rules and issue orders and guidance, as may be necessary or appropriate to enable the Bureau to administer and carry out the purposes and objectives of the Federal consumer financial laws, and to prevent evasions thereof." | None | None |
| Section 1022(b)(3)(A) | "…by rule, may conditionally or unconditionally exempt any class of covered persons, service providers, or consumer financial products or services, from any provision of this title, or from any rule issued under this title, as the Bureau determines necessary or appropriate to carry out the purposes and objectives of this title, taking into consideration the factors in subparagraph (B)." | None | None |
| Section 1022(c)(4)(B) | "…may…require covered persons and service providers participating in consumer financial services markets to file with the Bureau, under oath or otherwise, in such form and within such reasonable period of time as the Bureau may prescribe by rule or order, annual or special reports, or answers in writing to specific questions, furnishing information described in paragraph (4), as necessary for the Bureau to fulfill the monitoring, assessment, and reporting responsibilities imposed by Congress." | None | None |

## Appendix. (Continued)

| Section | Text of the Provision | Other Agencies | Deadlines for Rules |
|---|---|---|---|
| Section 1022(c)(5) | "In order to assess whether a nondepository is a covered person, as defined in section 1002, the Bureau may require such nondepository to file with the Bureau, under oath or otherwise, in such form and within such reasonable period of time as the Bureau may prescribe by rule or order, annual or special reports, or answers in writing to specific questions." | None | None |
| Section 1022(c)(7)(A) | "…may prescribe rules regarding registration requirements applicable to a covered person, other than an insured depository institution, insured credit union, or related person." | None | None |
| Section 1024(b)(7)(C) | "…may prescribe rules regarding a person described in subsection (a)(1), to ensure that such persons are legitimate entities and are able to perform their obligations to consumers. Such requirements may include background checks for principals, officers, directors, or key personnel and bonding or other appropriate financial requirements." | None | None |
| Section 1027(b)(2) | "…may exercise rulemaking, supervisory, enforcement, or other authority under this title with respect to a person described in paragraph (1) when such person is (A) engaged in an activity of offering or providing any consumer financial product or service…or (B) otherwise subject to any enumerated consumer law or any law for which authorities are transferred under subtitle F or H…." | None | None |

| Section | Text of the Provision | Other Agencies | Deadlines for Rules |
| --- | --- | --- | --- |
| Section 1027(g)(3)(B)(iii) | "Subject to a request or response pursuant to clause (i) or clause (ii) by the agencies made under this subparagraph (Departments of the Treasury and Labor), the Bureau may exercise rulemaking authority, and may act to enforce a rule prescribed pursuant to such request or response, in accordance with the provisions of this title." | None | None |
| Section 1031(b) | "…may prescribe rules applicable to a covered person or service provider identifying as unlawful unfair, deceptive, or abusive acts or practices in connection with any transaction with a consumer for a consumer financial product or service, or the offering of a consumer financial product or service. Rules under this section may include requirements for the purpose of preventing such acts or practices." | None | None |
| Section 1032(a) | "…may prescribe rules to ensure that the features of any consumer financial product or service, both initially and over the term of the product or service, are fully, accurately, and effectively disclosed to consumers in a manner that permits consumers to understand the costs, benefits, and risks associated with the product or service, in light of the facts and circumstances." | None | None |
| Section 1057(d)(3) | "…an arbitration provision in a collective bargaining agreement shall be enforceable as to disputes arising under subsection (a)(4), unless the Bureau determines, by rule, that such provision is inconsistent with the purposes of this title." | None | None |
| Section 1071(a) (amending the Equal Credit Opportunity Act (15 U.S.C. 1691 et seq.)) | "…shall prescribe such rules and issue such guidance as may be necessary to carry out, enforce, and compile data pursuant to this section" (on small business data collection). | None | None |

## Appendix. (Continued)

| Section | Text of the Provision | Other Agencies | Deadlines for Rules |
|---|---|---|---|
| Section 1071(a) (amending the Equal Credit Opportunity Act (15 U.S.C. 1691 et seq.)) | "…by rule or order, may adopt exceptions to any requirement of this section (on small business data collection) and may, conditionally or unconditionally, exempt any financial institution or class of financial institutions from the requirements of this section, as the Bureau deems necessary or appropriate to carry out the purposes of this section." | None | None |
| Section 1076(b) | The Bureau should issue rules if it "determines through the study required under subsection (a) (on reverse mortgage transactions) that conditions or limitations on reverse mortgage transactions are necessary or appropriate for accomplishing the purposes and objectives of this title…." | None | Study must be conducted within one year of enactment (i.e., by July 21, 2011), but no deadline established for possible regulations. |
| Section 1088(a) (amending the Fair Credit Reporting Act (15 U.S.C. 1681 et seq.)) | Prohibits the treatment of information as a consumer report if it is disclosed as "…determined to be necessary and appropriate, by regulation or order, by the Bureau or the applicable State insurance authority (with respect to any person engaged in providing insurance or annuities)." | Rule to be issued by the Bureau or applicable state insurance authorities | None |
| Section 1088(a)(4)(B) (amending the Fair Credit Reporting Act (15 U.S.C. 1681 et seq.)) | "…may, after notice and opportunity for comment, prescribe regulations that permit transactions under paragraph (2) that are determined to be necessary and appropriate to protect legitimate operational, transactional, risk, consumer, and other needs…." | None | None |

| Section | Text of the Provision | Other Agencies | Deadlines for Rules |
|---|---|---|---|
| Section 1088(a)(10)(E) (amending the Fair Credit Reporting Act (15 U.S.C. 1681 et seq.)) | "…shall prescribe such regulations as are necessary to carry out the purposes of this title, except with respect to sections 615(e) and 628. The Bureau may prescribe regulations as may be necessary or appropriate to administer and carry out the purposes and objectives of this title, and to prevent evasions thereof or to facilitate compliance therewith." | None | None |
| Section 1089(4) (amending the Fair Debt Collection Practices Act (15 U.S.C. 1692 et seq.)) | "Except as provided in section 1029(a) of the Consumer Financial Protection Act of 2010, the Bureau may prescribe rules with respect to the collection of debts by debt collectors, as defined in this title." | None | None |
| Section 1093 (amending Title V of the Gramm-Leach-Bliley Act (15 U.S.C. 6801 et seq.)) | "…shall have authority to prescribe such regulations as may be necessary to carry out the purposes of this subtitle with respect to financial institutions and other persons subject to their respective jurisdiction under section 505 (and notwithstanding subtitle B of the Consumer Financial Protection Act of 2010), except that the Bureau of Consumer Financial Protection shall not have authority to prescribe regulations with respect to the standards under section 501." | Bureau and the Securities and Exchange Commission authorized to issue rules | None |

## Appendix. (Continued)

| Section | Text of the Provision | Other Agencies | Deadlines for Rules |
|---|---|---|---|
| Section 1094 (amending the Home Mortgage Disclosure Act of 1975 (12 U.S.C. 2801 et seq.)) | "…may, by regulation, exempt from the requirements of this title any State-chartered repository institution within any State or subdivision thereof, if the agency determines that, under the law of such State or subdivision, that institution is subject to requirements that are substantially similar to those imposed under this title, and that such law contains adequate provisions for enforcement." | None | None |
| Section 1097(1) (amending Section 626 of the Omnibus Appropriations Act, 2009 (15 U.S.C. 1638 note)). | "…shall have authority to prescribe rules with respect to mortgage loans in accordance with section 553 of title 5, United States Code. Such rulemaking shall relate to unfair or deceptive acts or practices regarding mortgage loans, which may include unfair or deceptive acts or practices involving loan modification and foreclosure rescue services." | None | None |
| Section 1100(6)(B) (amending the S.A.F.E. Mortgage Licensing Act of 2008 (12 U.S.C. 5101 et seq.)) | "…is authorized to promulgate regulations setting minimum net worth or surety bond requirements for residential mortgage loan originators and minimum requirements for recovery funds paid into by loan originators." | None | None |

| Section | Text of the Provision | Other Agencies | Deadlines for Rules |
|---|---|---|---|
| Section 1472(a) (amending Chapter 2 of the Truth in Lending Act (15 U.S.C. 1631 et seq.)) | "…may jointly issue rules, interpretive guidelines, and general statements of policy with respect to acts or practices that violate appraisal independence in the provision of mortgage lending services for a consumer credit transaction secured by the principal dwelling of the consumer and mortgage brokerage services for such a transaction, within the meaning of subsections (a), (b), (c), (d), (e), (f), (h), and (i)." | Rule to be issued jointly with the Board of Governors, the Comptroller of the Currency, the Federal Deposit Insurance Corporation, the National Credit Union Administration Board, and the Federal Housing Finance Agency. | Per Section 1400(c), final rule to be published within 18 months after designated transfer date, and to take effect within 12 months after issuance. |
| Section 1472(a) (amending Chapter 2 of the Truth in Lending Act (15 U.S.C. 1631 et seq.)) | "…may jointly issue regulations that address the issue of appraisal report portability, including regulations that ensure the portability of the appraisal report between lenders for a consumer credit transaction secured by a 1-4 unit single family residence that is the principal dwelling of the consumer, or mortgage brokerage services for such a transaction." | Rule to be issued jointly with the Board of Governors, the Comptroller of the Currency, the Federal Deposit Insurance Corporation, the National Credit Union Administration Board, and the Federal Housing Finance Agency. | Per Section 1400(c), final rule to be published within 18 months after designated transfer date, and to take effect within 12 months after issuance. |

Source: CRS.

If the Council's action to stay or set aside a Bureau rule is itself a rule, then it would have to be submitted to GAO and both houses of Congress before it could take effect, and Congress could use the expedited procedures in the CRA to disapprove of the Council's action. On the other hand, if the Council's action is not a rule, then Congress would have to use regular legislative procedures to revoke the Council's action, or to put the Bureau's revoked rule into law.

## End Notes

[1] For more information on the Dodd-Frank Act, see CRS Report R41350, The Dodd-Frank Wall Street Reform and Consumer Protection Act: Issues and Summary, coordinated by Baird Webel.

[2] For more information, see CRS Report R41338, The Dodd-Frank Wall Street Reform and Consumer Protection Act: Title X, The Consumer Financial Protection Bureau, by David H. Carpenter.

[3] Section 1001.

[4] For more detailed information on Title X of the act, see CRS Report R41338, The Dodd-Frank Wall Street Reform and Consumer Protection Act: Title X, The Consumer Financial Protection Bureau, by David H. Carpenter.

[5] The relevant categories include "larger depositories" (those with more than $10 billion in assets), "smaller depositories (those with $10 billion or less in assets), and certain covered "nondepositories."

[6] For example, the CFPB will not have primary supervisory and enforcement powers over smaller depositories, but will be able to participate in examinations conducted by the institutions' prudential regulators, and can refer potential enforcement actions to their prudential regulators.

[7] Section 1100D. This section amended a statutory listing of independent regulatory agencies (44 U.S.C. 3502(5)), which includes such financial regulatory agencies as the Board of Governors of the Federal Reserve System, the Commodity Futures Trading Commission, and the Securities and Exchange Commission.

[8] See, for example, Paul R. Verkuil, "The Purposes and Limits of Independent Agencies," Duke Law Journal, vol. 37 (April-June 1988), pp. 257-279; and Marshall J. Breger and Gary J. Edles, "Established by Practice: The Theory and Operation of Independent Federal Agencies," Administrative Law Review, vol. 52 (2000), pp. 1111-1294.

[9] Section 1011(c).

[10] Section 1017.

[11] See Section 1062 for more information on the designated transfer date. The Secretary is required to determine the transfer date "in consultation with the Chairman of the Board of Governors, the Chairperson of the Corporation, the Chairman of the Federal Trade Commission, the Chairman of the National Credit Union Administration Board, the Comptroller of the Currency, the Director of the Office of Thrift Supervision, the Secretary of the Department of Housing and Urban Development, and the Director of the Office of Management and Budget."

[12] Section 1062(c). The Secretary can designate a transfer date later than 12 months after the date of enactment if Congress is provided a written notice and explanation, but in no case can the date be later than 18 months after the date of enactment.

[13] Section 1017(a)(3). As noted later in this report, Section 1002(14) of the Dodd-Frank Act defines "Federal consumer financial law" as "the provisions of this title, the enumerated consumer laws, the laws for which authorities are transferred under subtitles F and H, and any rule or order prescribed by the Bureau under this title, an enumerated consumer law, or pursuant to the authorities transferred under subtitles F and H. The term does not include the Federal Trade Commission Act." The "enumerated consumer laws" are defined in subsection (12) as including the Alternative Mortgage Transaction Parity Act of 1982 (12 U.S.C. 3801 et seq.); the Consumer Leasing Act of 1976 (15 U.S.C. 1667 et seq.); the Electronic Fund Transfer Act (15 U.S.C. 1693 et seq.), except with respect to section 920 of that act; the Equal Credit Opportunity Act (15 U.S.C. 1691 et seq.); the Fair Credit Billing Act (15 U.S.C. 1666 et seq.); the Fair Credit Reporting Act (15 U.S.C. 1681 et seq.), except with respect to sections 615(e) and 628 of that act (15 U.S.C. 1681m(e), 1681w); the Home Owners Protection Act of 1998 (12 U.S.C. 4901 et seq.); and the Fair Debt Collection Practices Act (15 U.S.C. 1692 et seq.).

[14] Interim final rulemaking is a particular application of the "good cause" exception to the notice-and-comment requirements in the Administrative Procedure Act (5 U.S.C. 553) in which an agency publishes a final rule without a previous proposed rule, but with a post-promulgation opportunity for comment.

[15] Section 1400(a).

[16] See, for example, David Cho, "Geithner's Realm Grows as Overhaul Nears Finish," Washington Post, July 17, 2010, p. A1; Lorraine Mirabella, "Lawyers Await Regulations to Spring from Financial Reform," McClatchy-Tribune Business News, July 27, 2010; and Eric Lichtblau, "Ex-Regulators Lobby to Shape Overhaul," New York Times, July 28, 2010, p. B1.

[17] See, for example, Jim Puzzanghera, "Wall Street Nervous About Watchdog's Bite; A Leading Candidate to Head a New Consumer Protection Agency Has Powerful Enemies," Los Angeles Times, p. A1; and Eileen Mozinski Schmidt, "Finance Leaders Wary of New Law," Telegraph-Herald, July 29, 2010, p. A-1, which said that "top of mind for many is how the new federal consumer-protection agency will develop and who will run it."

[18] Davis Polk & Wardwell, LLP, "Summary of the Dodd-Frank Wall Street Reform and Consumer Protection Act, Enacted into Law on July 21, 2010," available at http://www.davispolk.com/files/Publication/7084f9fe-6580-413bb870-b7c025ed2ecf/Presentation/PublicationAttachment/1d4495c7-0be0-4e9a-ba77-f786fb90464a/ 070910_Financial_Reform_Summary.pdf.

[19] For example, the Chamber of Commerce's Center for Capital Markets Competitiveness said that the Dodd-Frank Act "will lead to 520 rulemakings." See Thomas Quaadman, "Dodd-Frank: Governance Issues Galore and Not Limited to Financial Institutions, the Metropolitan Corporate Counsel, August 2010, p. 18, available at http://www.metrocorpcounsel.com/current.php?artType=view&artMonth=August&artYear=2010&EntryNo=11258.

[20] Titles X and XIV also require other agencies to issue regulations.

[21] Section 1002(14).

[22] The definition of "enumerated consumer laws" is in Section 1002(12).

[23] Section 1022(b)(2)(A).

[24] Section 1022(b)(2)(B) and (C).

[25] The exception is in Section 1061(b)(5), involving the authority of the Federal Trade Commission under the Federal Trade Commission Act.

[26] Section 1022(b)(4).

[27] Section 1022(c).

[28] Section 1022(c)(4)(B)(ii).

[29] Section 1022(c)(5). If these reports or answers meet the definition of a "collection of information" in the Paperwork Reduction Act (PRA), then they will have to be reviewed by the Office of Management and Budget before the information can be collected. The PRA (44 U.S.C. 3502(3)) defines "collection of information" as "the obtaining, causing to be obtained, soliciting, or requiring the disclosure to third parties or the public, of facts or opinions by or for an agency, regardless of form or format, calling for...answers to identical questions posed to, or identical reporting or recordkeeping requirements imposed on, ten or more persons, other than agencies, instrumentalities, or employees of the United States." For more information, see CRS Report R40636, Paperwork Reduction Act (PRA): OMB and Agency Responsibilities and Burden Estimates, by Curtis W. Copeland and Vanessa K. Burrows.

[30] These registration and disclosures may also be covered by the PRA's information collection and dissemination requirements. See 44 U.S.C. 3506(c) (for agency information collection requirements) and 44 U.S.C. 3506(d) (for agency information dissemination requirements).

[31] Section 1022(c)(3)(A).

[32] Section 1022(c)(6)(A) requires the Bureau to "prescribe rules regarding the confidential treatment of information obtained from persons in connection with the exercise of its authorities under Federal consumer financial law."

[33] The public may also be informed of upcoming rules through advance notices of proposed rulemaking, and through entries in the Unified Agenda of Federal Regulatory and Deregulatory Actions.

[34] The act does not specify what types of rules are to be considered "significant," presumably leaving these determinations to the Bureau.

[35] Section 553 of Title 5 generally requires federal agencies to publish a notice of proposed rulemaking, take comments on the proposed rule, develop a final rule taking those comments into consideration, and publish a final rule that cannot take effect until 30 days after the rule is published in the Federal Register. Even in the absence of this provision, these "notice and comment" requirements would generally apply to most of the rules that the Bureau is required or authorized to issue.

[36] 15 U.S.C. 1681m(h)(6)(B).

[37] Section 1041(c)(3).

[38] The only Title XIV provision that does not require that regulations be jointly issued is in Section 1463(a) (amending Section 6 of the Real Estate Settlement Procedures Act of 1974 (12 U.S.C. 2605)).

[39] Section 1011.

[40] For more information on these and other rulemaking statutes, see CRS Report RL32240, The Federal Rulemaking Process: An Overview, by Curtis W. Copeland.

[41] For more information on the operation of the Congressional Review Act, see CRS Report RL30116, Congressional Review of Agency Rulemaking: An Update and Assessment of The Congressional Review Act after a Decade, by Morton Rosenberg. See also CRS Report RL31160, Disapproval of Regulations by Congress: Procedure Under the Congressional Review Act, by Richard S. Beth.

[42] See CRS Report RL 34354, Congressional Influence on Rulemaking and Regulation Through Appropriations Restrictions, by Curtis W. Copeland.

[43] The President, Executive Order 12866, "Regulatory Planning and Review," 58 Federal Register51735, October 4, 1993, Section 6(a). A "significant" regulatory action is defined in Section 3(f) as "Any regulatory action that is likely to result in a rule that may (1) have an annual effect on the economy of $100 million or more or adversely affect in a material way the economy, a sector of the economy, productivity, competition, jobs, the environment, public health or safety, or State, local, or tribal governments or communities; (2) create a serious inconsistency or otherwise interfere with an action taken or planned by another agency; (3) materially alter the budgetary impact of entitlements, grants, user fees, or loan programs or the rights and obligations of recipients thereof; or (4) raise novel legal or policy issues arising out of legal mandates, the President's priorities, or the principles set forth in the Executive order." For more information on OIRA and its review process, see CRS Report RL32397, Federal Rulemaking: The Role of the Office of Information and Regulatory Affairs, by Curtis W. Copeland.

[44] Section 1(b)(6) of Executive Order 12866. As the executive order and OMB Circular A-4 make clear, even under this standard, the monetized benefits of a rule are not required to exceed the monetized costs of the rule before the agency can issue the rule, only that the costs of the rule be "justified" by the benefits (quantitative or non-quantitative).

[45] Section 6(a)(3)(C) of Executive Order 12866.

[46] Section 6(a)(3)(C)(iii) of Executive Order 12866.

[47] 44 U.S.C. 3508.

[48] 5 U.S.C. 553.

[49] 5 U.S.C. 553(b)(3(B). These requirements also do not apply to interpretative rules, general statements of policy, or rules of agency organization, procedure, or practice (5 U.S.C. 553(b)(A).

[50] 5 U.S.C. 553(d).

[51] For more information on the RFA, see CRS Report RL34355, The Regulatory Flexibility Act: Implementation Issues and Proposed Reforms, by Curtis W. Copeland.

[52] Agencies' interpretations of these phrases are, however, subject to judicial review (5 U.S.C. 611).

[53] See 5 U.S.C. 603(a), which states that agencies must prepare initial regulatory flexibility analyses "whenever an agency is required...to publish a general notice of proposed rulemaking for any proposed rule." See also 5 U.S.C. 604(a), which requires agencies to prepare a final regulatory flexibility analysis when an agency publishes a final rule "after being required...to publish a general notice of proposed rulemaking."

[54] Certain planning requirements in Section 4(b) and Section 4(c) regarding the "unified regulatory agenda" and the "regulatory plan" apply to independent regulatory agencies. Generally, however, the executive order does not apply to independent regulatory agencies.

[55] 44 U.S.C. 3507(f)(1).

[56] See, for example, U.S. General Accounting Office, Unfunded Mandates: Analysis of Reform Act Coverage, GAO-04-637, May 12, 2004.

[57] Section 1017. However, if the director of the CFPB determines that these unappropriated funds are insufficient, the Dodd-Frank Act authorizes appropriations of up to $200 million per year for FY2010 through FY2014. Appropriations restrictions could be added to any such appropriated funds.

[58] 5 U.S.C. 609.

[59] Section 1023(a).

[60] The Office of Financial Research was established by Section 152 of the Dodd-Frank Act.

[61] The Federal Insurance Office was established by Section 502 of the Dodd-Frank Act.

[62] Because only agencies who are "represented by members of the Council" can file petitions to stay or set aside rules, the member appointed by the President does not appear able to file a petition, since this member is supposed to be "independent" and does not represent an agency on the Council.

[63] Section 1023(c)(1). Section 102(a)(3) defines a "member agency" as a voting member of the Council

[64] Section 1023(c)(3).

[65] Section 1023(c)(4).

[66] Section 1023(c)(8).

[67] For more information on the operation of the Congressional Review Act, see CRS Report RL30116, Congressional Review of Agency Rulemaking: An Update and Assessment of The Congressional Review Act after a Decade, by Morton Rosenberg.

[68] The recent experience of rules issued pursuant to the recent health care reform legislation is instructive in this regard. The Patient Protection and Affordable Care Act (PPACA, P.L. 111-148, March 23, 2010) contained more than 40 provisions that required, permitted, or otherwise mentioned rulemaking. However, of the 10 final rules issued during the first four months of PPACA's implementation, 7 of them were not specifically required or mentioned in the act. See CRS Report R41346, PPACA Regulations Issued During the First Four Months of the Act's Implementation, by Curtis W. Copeland.

[69] In Sierra Club v. Costle (657 F.2d 298, D.C. Cir. 1981), the D.C. Circuit concluded (at 409) that it was "entirely proper for congressional representatives vigorously to represent the interests of their constituents before administrative agencies engaged in informal, general policy rulemaking, so long as the individual Members of Congress do not frustrate the intent of Congress as a whole as expressed in statute, nor undermine applicable rules of procedure."

[70] Dominique Custos, "The Rulemaking Power of Independent Regulatory Agencies," The American Journal of Comparative Law, vol. 54 (Fall 2006), p. 633.

[71] Joint statement of House and Senate Sponsors, 142 Cong. Rec. E571, at E571 (daily ed. April 19, 1996); 142 Cong. Rec. S3683, at S3683 (daily ed. April 18, 1996).

[72] If a rule is considered "major" (e.g., has a $100 million annual effect on the economy), then the CRA generally prohibits it from taking effect until 60 days after the date that it is submitted to Congress.

[73] For a detailed discussion of CRA procedures, see CRS Report RL31160, Disapproval of Regulations by Congress: Procedure Under the Congressional Review Act, by Richard S. Beth.

[74] For more on the potential scope of the definition of a "rule" under the CRA, see CRS Report RL30116, Congressional Review of Agency Rulemaking: An Update and Assessment of The Congressional Review Act after a Decade, by Morton Rosenberg.

[75] The rule overturned in March 2001 was the Occupational Safety and Health Administration's ergonomics standard. This reversal was the result of a unique set of circumstances in which the incoming President (George W. Bush) did not veto the resolution disapproving the outgoing President's (William J. Clinton's) rule. See CRS Report RL30116, Congressional Review of Agency Rulemaking: An Update and Assessment of The Congressional Review Act after a Decade, by Morton Rosenberg, for a description of several possible factors affecting the CRA's use, and for other effects that the act may have on agency rulemaking.

[76] See CRS Report RL30116, Congressional Review of Agency Rulemaking: An Update and Assessment of The Congressional Review Act after a Decade, by Morton Rosenberg, for a description of instances in which the filing of a resolution of disapproval had an effect on agencies' decisions.

In: The Consumer Financial Protection Bureau ISBN 978-1-62257-637-1
Editors: P. J. Cerutti and M. Kolchak 

*Chapter 5*

# FINANCIAL REPORT OF THE CONSUMER FINANCIAL PROTECTION BUREAU*

*Consumer Financial Protection Bureau*

## MESSAGE FROM THE SPECIAL ADVISOR TO THE SECRETARY OF THE TREASURY FOR THE CONSUMER FINANCIAL PROTECTION BUREAU

* This is an edited, reformatted and augmented version of Consumer Financial Protection Bureau, dated December 2011.

The Consumer Financial Protection Bureau (CFPB) was launched on July 21, 2011 with a focused goal: To make the markets for consumer financial products work for consumers, responsible providers, and the economy as a whole. We want to make sure that the price and risks of financial products are clear so that consumers can decide what products are best for them. And we want to make sure that there are sensible rules of the road and a level playing field so that providers can innovate and compete fairly.

The CFPB was created on July 21, 2010 by the Dodd-Frank Wall Street Reform and Consumer Protection Act. Before the Dodd-Frank Act, responsibility for administering and enforcing the various federal consumer financial laws was scattered across seven different federal agencies. For each of those seven agencies, consumer protection was only one of its responsibilities. The result was that no single agency was truly on the hook for protecting the average, everyday user of financial products and services. There was no true accountability, and consumers got left behind. The Dodd-Frank Act changed this by creating in the CFPB a single point of accountability for consumer financial protection. And we have been given, for the first time at the Federal level, supervisory authority over independent nonbank companies in addition to depositories. That means, for example, that when it comes to the mortgage market, we will be able to ensure that brokers, originators, and servicers play by the same rules regardless of their charter. It doesn't matter if you're a thrift, bank, finance company, ILC, or investment bank. If you want to be in the business of consumer finance, then you've got to play by the same rules as everybody else.

We recognize that the CFPB has a tough job. But fortunately, we have lots of tools in our toolkit – research, supervision, rulemaking, enforcement, and consumer education. Having the full range of tools means that we don't have to force a square policy peg into a round hole. We will strive to use each of these tools in the smartest way possible, matching problems to solutions.

Ultimately, our efforts will benefit the entire economy. We will help give families the confidence they need to borrow for a home or a child's education. We will help give our nation's financial institutions the confidence they need to innovate and compete. If we succeed in our mission, everybody wins.

As required by the Dodd-Frank Act, the CFPB prepared financial statements for fiscal year 2011.

The Government Accountability Office (GAO) rendered an unqualified -- or "clean" -- audit opinion on the CFPB's financial statements. GAO noted no material weaknesses or significant deficiencies in CFPB's internal controls and cited no instances of noncompliance with laws and regulations.

I am proud of the CFPB's first Financial Report. It describes the fiscal year 2011 efforts to establish the CFPB, and the results we have achieved to date. I am even more proud to be a part of the CFPB team, whose dedicated public service is making the promise of our mission a reality.

Raj Date
Special Advisor to the Secretary of the Treasury
for the Consumer Financial Protection Bureau

# PART A. MANAGEMENT'S DISCUSSION AND ANALYSIS

## Mission

The Consumer Financial Protection Bureau is a ***21st century agency*** that helps consumer financial markets work by making rules more effective, by consistently and fairly enforcing those rules, and by empowering consumers to take more control over their economic lives.

We will achieve our mission through...

- data-driven analysis
- innovative use of technology
- valuing the best people and great teamwork.

## I. Introduction

Beginning in 2007, the United States faced the most severe financial crisis since the Great Depression. Millions of Americans saw their home values drop, their savings shrink, their jobs eliminated, and their small businesses lose financing. Credit dried up, and countless consumer loans – many improperly made to begin with – went into default.

Many Americans took on loans that they did not fully understand and could not afford. Although some borrowers knowingly took on too much debt, many Americans who behaved responsibly were also lured into unaffordable loans by misleading promises of low payments. Honest lenders that resisted the pressure to sell complicated products had to compete with their less responsible competitors.

Even those who avoided the temptations of excessively risky credit were caught in its web. Those who never took out an unaffordable mortgage nonetheless saw the values of their homes plummet when neighbors lost homes in foreclosure. Those who used credit cards and home equity lines of credit judiciously saw across-the-board increases in interest rates on credit cards and contraction of outstanding lines of credit. Those who had saved regularly watched their retirement funds lose significant value. Cities and states cut back on services to make up for their own revenue losses. The cost of irresponsible lending has been and continues to be borne by tens of millions of American families.

In June 2009, President Obama proposed to address failures of consumer protection by establishing a new financial agency to focus directly on consumer protection. This new agency would heighten government accountability by consolidating in one place responsibilities that had been scattered across government. The agency would also have responsibility for supervising providers of consumer financial products and services that had not had regular federal oversight and for enforcing the consumer protection laws with respect to such providers. This agency would protect families from unfair, deceptive, and abusive financial practices. The President urged Congress to give the CFPB the same accountability and independence that the other banking agencies have and sufficient funding so it could ensure that financial companies would comply with consumer laws.

In July 2010, Congress passed and President Obama signed the Dodd-Frank Wall Street Reform and Consumer Protection Act. The law – often referred to as the Dodd-Frank Act – created the Bureau of Consumer Financial Protection (also known as the "Consumer Financial Protection Bureau" or the "CFPB"). Part of the purpose of creating the CFPB was to increase accountability in government by consolidating consumer financial protection authorities that had existed across seven different federal agencies into one. Instead of important consumer protection powers being scattered across the federal government, now a single entity would have the oversight authority to make sure consumer financial markets work for all consumers.

## II. Establishment of the Consumer Financial Protection Bureau

One of the key elements of the Dodd-Frank Act was the creation of a new financial regulatory agency, the CFPB, which centralizes consumer protection authorities and increases accountability for the supervision and enforcement of laws governing consumer financial products and services. Specifically, the agency is tasked with protecting consumers from unfair, deceptive, and abusive financial practices by making the markets for consumer financial products and services work for American families.

The Dodd-Frank Act created the CFPB as an independent bureau within the Federal Reserve System. The CFPB is an Executive agency as defined in section 105 of Title 5, United States Code. Title X of the Dodd-Frank Act established the following goals for the CFPB:

- Ensure that consumers have timely and understandable information to make responsible decisions about financial transactions,
- Protect consumers from unfair, deceptive, or abusive acts or practices, and from discrimination,
- Reduce outdated, unnecessary, or overly burdensome regulations,
- Promote fair competition by enforcing the federal consumer financial laws consistently, and
- Encourage markets for consumer financial products and services that operate transparently and efficiently to facilitate access and innovation.

Under the Dodd-Frank Act, the Secretary of the Treasury is responsible for exercising the CFPB authorities until a Director of the Bureau is in place. On July 18, 2011 President Obama sent to the Senate a nomination for a Director of the CFPB. Until confirmed by the Senate, the day-to-day operations of the CFPB are being managed by the Special Advisor to the Secretary of the Treasury for the CFPB.

## III. CFPB Stand-Up Actions and Status

CFPB leadership recognize that they have a unique and vital opportunity to create an organization with an innovative infrastructure, and accordingly, articulated a mission and vision and began establishing the infrastructure, tools and processes to attract, hire, develop and retain the human capital needed to build an agency responsible for protecting consumers of financial products and services. The tools needed by the CFPB to begin hiring, compensating, and managing employees using the CFPB's own statutory authorities under the Dodd-Frank Act were put in place and became operational in February 2011.

The CFPB has currently filled 25 of its key leadership positions with highly talented and experienced staff from the private, nonprofit, and public sectors. In addition, the CFPB has made considerable progress in recruiting, hiring, and orienting the workforce.

The CFPB's recruitment efforts have focused on filling vacancies throughout the country in support of its headquarters operations in Washington, D.C., and its regional satellite offices in Chicago, New York City, and San Francisco.

In addition, to ensure the successful stand-up of the Bureau, CFPB staff conducted reviews of "best practices" and "lessons learned" from the merger and stand-up of other federal agencies. The team also solicited input on stand-up needs and issues from other government agencies, private corporations, and the public. As a result of this process, staff used the following principles to guide the development and implementation of the CFPB's organization and human capital strategies:

- Focus on the CFPB's core principles and priorities (see below) to guide the organizational design and stand-up,
- Establish clear implementation goals and timelines that build momentum and demonstrate progress,
- Establish and implement a communication strategy to create shared expectations and report progress, and
- Build a "learning organization" that provides for the continuing development and advancement of the Bureau.

The CFPB has also implemented an initial workforce design strategy that identifies the human capital assets necessary to accomplish the CFPB's mission in line with the CFPB's vision and core organizational principles and priorities. This strategy has served to guide recruiting efforts to date and continues to serve as the CFPB's long-range workforce vision.

***Organization***

One of the Bureau's top priorities has been to build an organization for success using a design that will provide the infrastructure the Bureau needs to meet its responsibilities. Late last calendar year, the CFPB began providing its draft organization chart to Members of Congress and the media. In early February 2011, the Bureau posted the chart to its newly launched website. In developing the CFPB's organizational structure, the Bureau has asked for comments and critiques from stakeholders across the spectrum. The CFPB organization chart as of September 30, 2011 is displayed below:

**The CFPB's Core Organizational Principles and Priorities**

**Engage** the American public.

**Ensure** that federal consumer financial laws are administered consistently, efficiently, and effectively.

**Help** create a level playing field for community banks and credit unions to compete with large banks and non-depository financial companies.

**Make** the CFPB a data-driven agency by ensuring research and market analysis are at the core of all of its work.

**Advance** financial education opportunities for all Americans.

**Continue** an open and candid dialogue with Members of Congress.

**Strengthen** accountability within the CFPB.

The Bureau currently includes six primary divisions:

- Consumer Education and Engagement
- Supervision, Enforcement, Fair Lending and Equal Opportunity
- Research, Markets, and Regulations
- Office of General Counsel
- External Affairs
- Office of Chief Operating Officer

A description of the functions and responsibilities of the each of the Divisions follows.

**Consumer Education and Engagement**

Provides, through a variety of initiatives and methods, information to consumers that will allow them to make decisions that are best for them. Consumer education is a central mission to the Bureau. The Bureau is developing targeted outreach to groups that face particular challenges, as required by the Dodd-Frank Act.

It includes the following offices:

*Community Affairs* – conducts outreach to consumer groups, civil rights groups, community organizations, and other organizations focused on traditionally underserved consumers and communities.

*Consumer Engagement* – creates engaging experiences for the American public to enable them to live better financial lives and for people interacting with the Bureau by developing platforms for participatory government.

*Financial Education* – serves as a resource for consumers who are looking to better understand how to make decisions in the financial services marketplace and provides access to tools and information that can help consumers make financial choices.

*Older Americans* – helps prevent financial abuse of seniors, promotes consumer education and consumer protection efforts, and develops initiatives to ensure appropriate tools are available to guide financial decision making for Americans 65 and over.

*Servicemember Affairs* – works in partnership with the Department of Defense to (1) help ensure that military families receive the financial education they need to make the best financial decisions for them; (2) monitor complaints from military families, and responses to those complaints; and (3) coordinate the efforts of federal and state agencies to improve consumer financial protection measures for military families.

*Students* – assesses and develops policy and educational solutions to address and prevent consumer financial protection issues of students.

**Supervision, Enforcement, Fair Lending and Equal Opportunity**

Ensures compliance with federal consumer financial laws by supervising market participants and bringing enforcement actions when appropriate.

It includes the following offices:

*Bank Supervision* – conducts examinations of the largest and most complex banks, thrifts, and credit unions in the country, as well as other depository institutions under the Bureau's jurisdiction. These efforts are closely coordinated with the Nonbank Supervision office.

*Enforcement* – initiates investigations and enforcement actions, where appropriate, to ensure that providers of consumer financial products and services are complying with the law and that such providers are held accountable when they fail to do so.

*Fair Lending and Equal Opportunity* – provides oversight and enforcement of fair lending laws to make certain that credit decisions are not based on race or any other prohibited factor. The office also engages in fair lending outreach and education.

*Nonbank Supervision* - conducts examinations of different types of nonbank consumer financial services companies, including nonbank affiliates of large depository institutions.

## Research, Markets and Regulations

Responsible for understanding consumer financial markets and consumer behavior and for evaluating whether there is a need for regulation and the costs and benefits of potential or existing regulations. Before the CFPB acts, it will seek to be fully informed. The offices within this division are staffed with professionals selected for their strong analytical skills and subject matter expertise.

It includes the following offices:

*Research* – conducts research and rigorous policy evaluations and publishes findings on a variety of topics to support the CFPB's evidence-based policymaking and to develop a deeper understanding of consumer financial markets and household finances.

*Market teams* – provide real-time market intelligence, guidance, and analysis of their respective consumer markets. The market teams are Cards Markets, Mortgage Markets, Installment & Liquidity Lending Markets, and Deposits, Collections & Credit Information Markets.

*Regulations* – works to ensure that rulemaking is conducted in an informed, fair, and efficient manner in accordance with the law.

## Office of General Counsel

Responsible for the CFPB's compliance with all applicable laws and provides advice to the Director and CFPB's divisions.

**External Affairs**

Responsible for ensuring that the CFPB maintains robust dialogue with various stakeholders who have an interest in its work in order to promote understanding, transparency, and accountability.

It includes the following offices:

*Community Banks and Credit Unions* - conducts outreach to smaller credit providers, especially community banks and credit unions.

*Consumer Advisory Board* - advises and consults with the Bureau in the exercise of its functions and provides information on emerging practices in the consumer financial products or services industry, including regional trends and concerns.

*Intergovernmental Affairs* - conducts outreach to municipal, state, and other government entities with coinciding concerns or initiatives.

*Legislative Affairs* - serves a liaison function with the Members of Congress and congressional staff, providing timely information on the Bureau's activities and responding to inquiries and concerns.

*Media Relations* - serves a liaison function with the media.

*Ombudsman* - focuses on problem resolution between the CFPB and regulated entities or other third parties.

**Office of Chief Operating Officer**

Builds and sustains the CFPB's operational infrastructure to support the entire organization and includes the Offices of the Chief Financial Officer; Chief Information Officer; Chief Technology Officer; and Chief Human Capital Officer; Minority and Women Inclusion Office; Operations and Facilities; Procurement; and FOIA, Privacy and Records. This division also includes Consumer Response, which receives complaints and helps consumers find answers for questions about consumer financial products and services.

***On-Board Status***

One of the key areas of focus in building the CFPB has been to identify the best qualified people to meet its immediate staffing needs. The CFPB has made significant strides by transferring[1] or hiring approximately 663 highly qualified personnel by September 30, 2011. This progress has been accomplished by taking many concurrent steps in the areas of policy development, recruitment activities, development of metrics, and on-boarding these many new employees, all within very compressed time frames.

Provided below is a chart that displays the dramatic quarterly growth of on-board positions filled for the CFPB during fiscal year 2011.

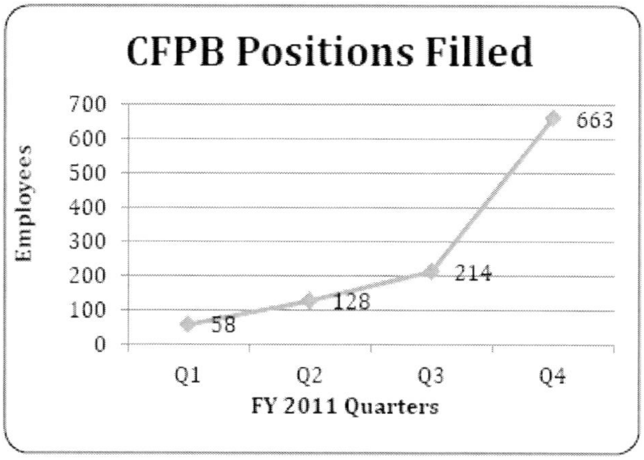


Provided below is a percentage breakout of CFPB total on-board staff by division as of September 30, 2011. As displayed in the chart, the CFPB's initial efforts to staff the bureau has placed a high priority on the Supervision, Enforcement, Fair Lending and Equal Opportunity functions – 51.9% of total on-board staff – receiving the highest attention in filling CFPB regulatory and compliance expertise positions.

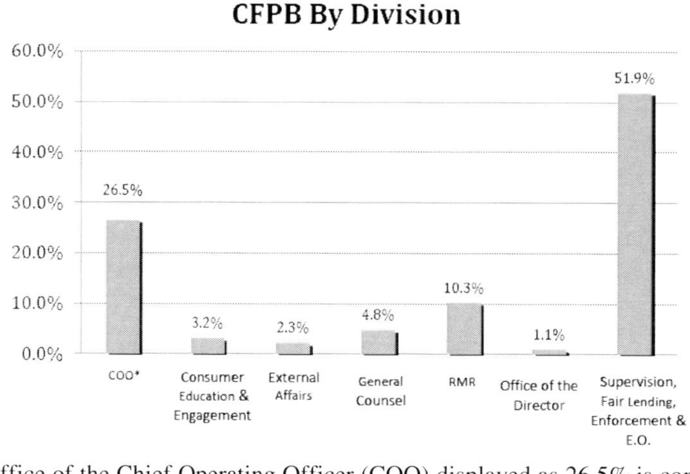


*The Office of the Chief Operating Officer (COO) displayed as 26.5% is composed of 12.5% for the Consumer Response Center and 14% for all other COO functions.

***Design and Implement Payroll and Human Resources Systems***

The Dodd-Frank Act did not give the CFPB direct-hire authority, and the CFPB was required to implement its own payroll and hiring system in order to begin hiring regulatory and compliance expertise – either from competitive hires or from transfer agencies. The CFPB launched a series of discussions and negotiations with the Federal Reserve System and with federal providers of payroll and human resource (HR) systems. The CFPB ultimately decided to implement an independent payroll and HR automated system separate from the systems used by the Federal Reserve.

Under the Dodd-Frank Act, the CFPB must establish a compensation program that provides compensation and benefits that, at a minimum, are comparable to the compensation and benefits being provided by the Board of Governors for the corresponding class of employees. All such compensation and benefits must be based on the terms and conditions set forth in the Federal Reserve Act. Accordingly, the CFPB undertook a complete compensation and classification analysis and developed a market-based classification and compensation system that supports its strategy of building a highly skilled, flexible, high-performing workforce and that attracts both individuals from outside of government as well as employees from the agencies transferring functions to the CFPB.

Additionally, the CFPB developed its own benefits program and implemented it on July 17, 2011. Pursuant to the Dodd-Frank Act, the CFPB has collaborated with the six transferring agencies[2] to establish procedures and systems that allow for employees transferring into the CFPB to retain appropriate benefits provided to them by their prior agency for a one-year period and to reimburse those agencies as required by the Dodd-Frank Act. The six agencies are the Department of Housing and Urban Development, Office of Thrift Supervision, Office of the Comptroller of the Currency, National Credit Union Administration, Federal Deposit Insurance Corporation, and the Federal Reserve Board of Governors and Federal Reserve System Banks.

## IV. CFPB Actions, Performance and Results

The Dodd-Frank Act under section 1062 required the transfer date of the consumer financial protection functions from the seven prudential Federal agencies[3] to occur no later than July 21, 2011 unless Congress was notified. The Senior Advisor to the Secretary of the Treasury and CFPB management established as the primary performance goal for fiscal year 2011 the establishment and stand-up of the CFPB by the transfer date of July 21, 2011.[4]

On July 21, 2011 the CFPB achieved its goal and began its work to carry out its responsibilities and authorities to enforce the laws on credit cards, mortgages, student loans, prepaid cards, and other kinds of financial products and services. Some of the CFPB actions starting that day include:

- The CFPB sent introductory letters to the CEOs of the depository institutions – generally large banks and their affiliates – that are subject to CFPB supervision. These letters, which outline the agency's approach to supervision and examination, marked the beginning of CFPB's regular communications with the institutions it supervises. In addition, CFPB's Enforcement team was ready to begin enforcing federal consumer financial laws, when necessary.
- The CFPB's Consumer Response Center began accepting credit card complaints on its newly redesigned website, and through a toll-free number. CFPB also began referring distressed homeowners to housing counselors via the Homeowner's mortgage assistance hotline.
- The CFPB began publishing regulations and interim rules, examples of which include: a list of the regulations of the transferor agencies that will be enforceable by the CFPB; interim rules to create records and information procedures to implement the Privacy Act and the Freedom of Information Act, and to establish a process by which parties may seek testimony or records from the CFPB for use in litigation; and an interim rule concerning the CFPB's conduct of investigations of potential violations of any provision of federal consumer financial law.

In addition, CFPB began work on many initiatives prior to July 21, 2011, including:

- **Know Before You Owe** – In May, the CFPB launched the Know Before You Owe project, an effort to combine two federally required mortgage disclosures into a single, simpler form that makes the costs and risks of the loan clear and allows consumers to comparison shop for the best offer. The CFPB began testing two alternate prototype forms that are designed to be given to consumers who have just applied for a mortgage loan. This testing – which is nearing completion and involves one-on-one interviews with consumers, lenders, and brokers which – will precede and inform the CFPB's formal rulemaking process. The CFPB also has posted the prototypes on its website with an interactive tool to gather public input about the designs.

- **Transparency in Credit Cards –** Credit cards are the most commonly used form of consumer credit. Almost two out of three families now have at least one credit card, and almost half of all families with credit cards carry a balance. In February 2011, the CFPB held a conference on the first anniversary of when many provisions of the Credit Card Accountability Responsibility and Disclosure Act – the CARD Act – took effect. The CFPB's conference brought together industry representatives, consumer groups, academics, government experts, and others for a review of data on how the CARD Act, coupled with the recession and its aftermath, have affected supply, demand, and pricing within the credit card marketplace. The CFPB undertook a voluntary survey of the nine largest card issuers, representing approximately 90 percent of the market, and other studies also were conducted in connection with the conference.

  The CARD Act has pushed in the right direction. It has brought about significant reforms in both the pricing practices of card issuers and the information provided to consumers. Even so, there are a lot of moving parts in a credit card price, and there is still room for improvement in the transparency of this market. The CFPB's next challenge will be to further clarify price and risk and make it easier for consumers to make direct product comparisons.

  As part of the CFPB's commitment to transparency, the raw data from a consumer survey conducted by the CFPB in connection with the conference were made public on its website at: www.consumer finance.gov

- **Report on Using Remittance History for Credit Scores and Remittance Exchange Rates** – Each year, consumers in the United States send tens of billions of dollars to family members, friends, businesses, and others abroad through remittance transfers – electronic transfers from U.S. senders to recipients in foreign countries. The CFPB issued a report on July 20, 2011 mandated by the Dodd-Frank Act, which analyzes two subjects related to remittance transfers: the transparency and disclosure to consumers of exchange rates used in remittance transfers, and the potential for using remittance histories to enhance the credit scores of consumers.

The report finds that implementation of some of the Dodd-Frank Act's new requirements related to remittance transfers – including mandatory disclosures of the exchange rate used – could shed light on any need for additional exchange rate transparency measures. The CFPB also recommends to policy makers and other stakeholders that any additional transparency measures be evaluated and considered together with the range of mechanisms for increasing the competitiveness of the remittance transfer market, or promoting other consumer protection goals. The report further discusses the potential for remittance histories to inform credit scores, and describes planned CFPB research regarding the relationship between remittance histories and credit scores.

- **Report on Credit Scores** – CFPB issued a mandated report on July 19, 2011 examining the differences between credit scores sold to consumers and scores used by lenders to make credit decisions.

  The Dodd-Frank Act required the CFPB to study the differences between credit scores consumers purchase and those creditors use to make credit decisions. The CFPB's report covers the process of developing credit scoring models, why different scoring models may produce different scores for the same consumer, how different scoring models are used by creditors in the marketplace, what credit scores are available to consumers for purchase, and ways that differences between the scores provided to creditors and those provided to consumers may disadvantage consumers. A consumer unaware of the variety of credit scores available in the market place may purchase a score believing it to be his or her only credit score, when in fact there is no such single score.

  The report discusses the general lack of information about credit scoring. One survey shows that many consumers do not know that a credit score represents the risk of not repaying a loan. Furthermore, many consumers do not know that credit scores they buy may not use the same credit scoring models that are most widely used by lenders.

  As a followup to the report, the CFPB will obtain and analyze data that shed further light on differences in scores and the significance of related concerns. To help educate consumers, the CFPB also posted advice on its website about how to obtain and maintain a good credit score: http://www.consumerfinance.gov.

- **Larger Participants and Nonbank Supervision** – The Dodd-Frank Act gives the CFPB the job of supervising large banks, as well as some other types of financial companies, for compliance with federal consumer financial protection laws. While banks, thrifts, and credit unions have been subject to examinations by various federal regulators in the past, other types of companies providing consumer financial products and services have not. One of the goals of the new law is to better protect consumers by expanding this type of supervision to nonbank companies. The examination of nonbank companies will be a crucial piece of the CFPB's work. For the first time, many of these nonbank financial companies will be subject to federal oversight.
  Under the Act, the CFPB's nonbank supervision program will be able to look at companies of all sizes in the mortgage, payday lending, and private student lending markets. But for all other markets—like consumer installment loans, money transmitting, and debt collection—the CFPB generally can supervise only larger participants.
  The CFPB requested input on June 29, 2011 on how to define a "larger participant" through the rulemaking process. In order to collect input, CFPB published a Notice and Request for Comment (Notice). Public comments on the questions listed in the Notice will help the CFPB formulate a rule that helps the CFPB make the best use of its resources to protect American consumers.

***Engaging the Public***

One of the CFPB's top priorities is to communicate substantively and frequently across a wide range of industry and consumer group sectors. The CFPB aims to actively engage all stakeholders that could potentially be affected by the agency, with the understanding that there is much insight to be gained from varied perspectives that represent many distinct points of view.

The CFPB has traveled across the country to listen to and learn from the hopes, fears, and concerns of industry and consumer groups. As a result, the CFPB has collected ample information about how its work will affect various stakeholders, and suggestions from stakeholders have informed preparations in setting up the agency.

- **Community Banks and Credit Unions** – CFPB set a goal to reach out to small independent banks in all 50 states before July 21, 2011.

By April 2011, the CFPB had reached its goal of speaking to bankers from every state. Further, CFPB officials delivered speeches at the Independent Community Bankers of America National Convention, the Credit Union National Association Governmental Affairs Conference, and at the National Association of Federal Credit Unions Congressional Caucus. A CFPB team has been dedicated to outreach to small financial service providers.

- **Trade Associations and Bank Executives** – CFPB has frequently met with banking executives and trade associations that represent both depository and non-depository institutions. The CFPB has spoken directly to many of the major trade organizations representing firms likely to be affected by its work and delivered speeches to the Financial Services Roundtable and at the U.S. Chamber of Commerce Fifth Annual Capital Market Summit.
- **Servicemembers and Military Families** – In January 2011, the CFPB made a key hire to establish its Office of Servicemember Affairs. The newly hired Assistant Director, Office of Servicemembers Affairs (OSA) understands – from personal experience as a military spouse and work at the Better Business Bureau Military Line – that men and women in the U.S. armed forces encounter unique financial issues.

  In January, the Assistant Director, OSA visited Joint Base San Antonio, Texas to speak with servicemembers and financial counselors about the unique financial circumstances and challenges that exist in military communities. In April, the Assistant Director traveled to Joint Base Myer-Henderson Hall in Virginia to meet with servicemembers and their families.

  The Assistant Director has visited many other military bases as well, talking about the financial challenges facing American men and women in uniform. The Assistant Director was the first CFPB staffer to testify before Congress when she appeared before the House Committee on Veterans Affairs and has also testified before a subcommittee of the Senate Committee on Homeland Security and Governmental Affairs, and has submitted testimony for the record to the Subcommittee on Federal Financial Management, Government Information, Federal Services and International Security U.S. Senate Committee on Homeland Security.
- **Consumer Response** – The Dodd-Frank Act directs the CFPB to facilitate the collection and monitoring of, and response to, consumer

complaints regarding certain financial products and services. These complaints and consumers' inquiries will help the CFPB identify areas of concern and help CFPB in its supervision and other responsibilities.

The CFPB is implementing the consumer response function gradually through a phased roll-out of functionality. The CFPB aims to build an efficient and effective consumer response system that is useful to American consumers, minimizes burden on financial institutions, and leverages the best of technology. A phased roll-out will enable proper consideration of the needs of consumers, the requirements of financial institutions, and the relevant operational constraints. In the initial phase, the CFPB will focus on taking complaints for credit cards, with other products to follow.

Anticipating that many distressed homeowners would contact the CFPB soon after the launch of the Consumer Response function, the CFPB designed a process to connect these homeowners with a housing counselor via the Homeowner's HOPETM Hotline, a housing counseling hotline available through the Department of the Treasury.

The CFPB is coordinating its approach with other regulators to prevent any gaps for consumers during this transition of responsibilities[3]. As the CFPB rolls out its full functionality, it plans to route or refer incoming complaints for other products to the prudential regulators or other appropriate agencies.

The CFPB is investing in a 21st-century IT infrastructure to ensure that its consumer response function is accessible, easy to use, and secure. To ensure broad access, the CFPB will provide a variety of contact channels, including the Internet, mail, fax, and a toll-free telephone number with English and Spanish language capabilities. For consumers, the CFPB is creating an integrated web and phone system to file and track complaints. The CFPB's website and call center will also provide answers to frequently asked questions regarding financial products. For credit card complaints, the CFPB is creating a web-based system that allows card issuers to log on, view, and respond to complaints online. Eventually, this system is expected to be used by providers of other financial products.

The CFPB has engaged and will continue to engage a broad range of stakeholders – including community banks, consumer advocates, industry groups, and others – to gather input on the complaint handling process. The CFPB has presented its complaint intake process and complaint handling system to the largest credit card issuers. The CFPB will be holding ongoing discussions with them regarding improvements to the system.

# V. Enterprise Risk Management

**Fiscal Year 2011**
**CFPB STATEMENT OF MANAGEMENT ASSURANCES**
**November 9, 2011**

The management of the Consumer Financial Protection Bureau (CFPB) is responsible for establishing and maintaining effective internal control and financial management systems that meet the objectives of the Federal Managers' Financial Integrity Act of 1982 (FMFIA). Continuous monitoring and periodic evaluations provide the basis for the annual assessment and report on management's controls, as required by FMFIA.

CFPB is leveraging the established OMB Circular A-123 and the FMFIA assessment methodologies to assist in assessing the applicable entity-wide controls, documenting the applicable processes, and identifying and testing the key controls.

Based on the results of these ongoing evaluations, CFPB can provide reasonable assurance that internal control over the effectiveness and efficiency of operations and compliance with applicable laws and regulations meet the objectives of FMFIA and no material weaknesses were found in the design or operation of the internal controls as of September 30, 2011.

As required by the Dodd-Frank Act, the CFPB is required to provide a management assertion as to the effectiveness of CFPB's internal control over financial reporting. CFPB management is responsible for establishing and maintaining effective internal control over financial reporting.

CFPB conducted its assessment of the effectiveness of internal control over financial reporting based on the criteria established under 31 U.S.C. Sec. 3512(c). Based on the results of this evaluation, the CFPB can provide reasonable assurance that its internal control over financial reporting as of September 30, 2011 was operating effectively and no material weaknesses were found in the design or operation of the internal control over financial reporting.

As required by the Dodd-Frank Act, the CFPB is required to maintain financial management systems that comply substantially with Federal financial management systems requirements and applicable Federal accounting standards. The CFPB utilizes financial management systems that substantially comply with the requirements for Federal financial management systems and applicable Federal accounting standards.

Raj Date
Special Advisor to the Secretary of the Treasury
for the Consumer Financial Protection Bureau

***Federal Managers' Financial Integrity Act***

The CFPB was established as an independent bureau in the Federal Reserve System under the Dodd-Frank Act Section 1011 (a). As an independent, non-appropriated bureau, CFPB recognizes the importance of Federal laws associated with implementing effective enterprise risk management, including the Federal Managers' Financial Integrity Act. This includes ensuring that CFPB operations and programs are effective and efficient and that internal controls are sufficient to minimize exposure to waste and mismanagement.

In fiscal year 2011, CFPB performed an evaluation of its risks and systems of internal controls and employed an independent accounting firm to assist CFPB management in its evaluations. The results of those evaluations helped to support the CFPB's reasonable assurance of effective internal control.

The CFPB is committed to ensuring it has an effective risk management program in fiscal year 2012 and will take actions to implement all identified recommendations and concerns, and increase resources assigned to an office within the Office of the Chief Financial Officer -- the Office of Audit and Internal Controls.

***Federal Financial Management Systems Requirements***

Section1017 (a) (4) (C) of the Dodd-Frank Act requires the CFPB to implement and maintain financial management systems that substantially comply with Federal financial management systems requirements and applicable Federal accounting standards. As discussed below in the section on Financial Management System Strategy, the CFPB has entered into an agreement with the Department of the Treasury's Bureau of Public Debt (BPD) for the cross-servicing of CFPB's core financial management system needs. As such, BPD has provided assurances to CFPB that its system is in compliance with the Federal Financial Management Improvement Act (FFMIA) whereby the system is substantially compliant with:

- Federal financial management system requirements,
- Applicable federal accounting standards, and
- The United States Standard General Ledger at the transaction level.

BPD has reported that its system substantially complies with the three requirements of FFMIA and recently completed a Statement on Standards for Attestation Engagement (SSAE) No. 16, Reporting on Controls at a Service Organization. The independent auditors opined in the SSAE-16 report that, in short, BPD's controls were suitably designed to provide reasonable assurance that control objectives would be achieved if customer agencies applied the complementary customer agency controls.

CFPB evaluated its internal controls over the processing of transactions between the CFPB and BPD. CFPB determined it has adequate complementary controls in place.

***Financial Statement Audit and Report on Internal Control over Financial Reporting***

Sections 1017 (a) (4) (B) and (D) of the Dodd-Frank Act require the CFPB to prepare and submit to GAO annual financial statements and an assertion of the effectiveness of the internal controls over financial reporting. Section 1017 (a) (5) (A) and (B) of the Dodd-Frank Act also require GAO to audit those financial statements and assertions and report their results to the bureau, Congress and the President. The CFPB prepared financial statements for the first full year of operation, fiscal year 2011.

GAO issued an unqualified audit opinion on CFPB's fiscal year 2011 financial statements GAO noted no material weaknesses or significant deficiencies in CFPB's internal controls and cited no instances of non-compliance with laws and regulations.

***Financial Management Systems Strategy***

CFPB recognized early on that as a new bureau it needed to leverage existing financial management resources, systems and information technology platforms when identifiable and available. Initially, all of CFPB's financial management transactions were processed through the Department of the Treasury's Departmental Offices. In fiscal year 2011, CFPB entered into a contract with the Department of the Treasury's Bureau of Public Debt (BPD) for the cross-servicing of a core financial management system that uses a commercial off-the-shelf core financial management system designed and configured to meet generally accepted accounting principles for Federal entities. In addition to the core financial management system, BPD provides additional services to CFPB, such as transactional processing, financial reporting, human resource services, procurement services, and travel services.

Further, CFPB established an IT Investment Review Board (IRB) as an executive advisory body providing the business and technology leadership to ensure all technology investment aligns with the CFPB mission and goals. The members of the IRB work with the CIO and the Technology Implementation Group to make informed recommendations and assist the CIO in making the proper investment decisions to ensure that CFPB's IT assets are managed as strategic business resources that support the mission of the bureau.

***Federal Information Security Management Act***

The Federal Information Security Management Act (FISMA) requires Federal agencies to develop, document, and implement an agency-wide program to provide security for the information and information systems that support the operations and assets of the agency. As discussed above, the CFPB has leveraged existing information technology and platforms by deploying a cloud-based infrastructure and entering into various cross-servicing agreements with the Department of the Treasury, Departmental Offices and BPD, and the Department of Agriculture, National Finance Center. As part of the independent performance audit of the operations and budget of the CFPB, which is discussed below, the auditors also reported that the CFPB has complied with key elements of the E-Government Act of 2002, including FISMA.

***Improper Payments Elimination and Recovery Act***

The Improper Payments Elimination and Recovery Act of 2011 require agencies to review their programs and activities annually to identify those susceptible to significant improper payments. During fiscal year 2011, the Office of Audit and Internal Control conducted such a review over four areas of payments – Purchase Card, Contract Payments and/or Invoices, Travel Card, and Claims and/or Vouchers. The CFPB's risk assessment process did not identify any programs susceptible to significant improper payments.

### *Independent Performance Audit of the Operations and Budget of the CFPB*

The Dodd-Frank Act, amended by the Full-Year Continuing Appropriations Act, 2011 (12 USC 5496a), mandated that CFPB obtain an annual independent audit of the operations and budget of the Bureau. CFPB contracted for a fiscal year 2011 independent performance audit of the CFPB budget and several operating areas that were instrumental in implementing the Dodd-Frank Wall Street Reform and Consumer Financial Protection Act of 2010 and standing up the CFPB: Human Capital and Organizational Development, Consumer Response, Information Technology, and Communications and Transparency.

To evaluate CFPB's operations and performance in these five areas, the auditor's evaluation criteria were (1) compliance with legal requirements, (2) achievement of organizational goals, and (3) alignment with performance standards, best practices, and/or benchmarks. In its October 15 report, the auditors reported that CFPB has made significant progress towards achieving legal compliance, attaining organizational goals, and meeting performance standards.

### *Limitations of the Financial Statements*

The principal financial statements contained in this report have been prepared to present the financial position and results of operations of the Consumer Financial Protection Bureau pursuant to the requirements of the Dodd-Frank Act Section 1017 (a) (4) (B). While the statements have been prepared from the books and records of the Consumer Financial Protection Bureau, in accordance with generally accepted accounting principles for the Federal government, and follows the general presentation guidance provided by OMB, the statements are in addition to the financial reports used to monitor and control budgetary resources, which are prepared using the same books and records. The statements should be read with the realization that they are for a component of the United States Government, a sovereign entity.

## VI. Financial Analysis

### *How the CFPB is Funded*

Under the Dodd-Frank Act, the CFPB is funded principally by transfers from the Board of Governors of the Federal Reserve System up to a limit set forth in the statute. The CFPB requests transfers from the Board of Governors in amounts that are reasonably necessary to carry out its mission, which funding is capped at a pre-set percentage of the total 2009 operating expenses of the Federal Reserve System, subject to an annual adjustment. Specifically, the CFPB fund transfers are capped as follows:

- In fiscal year 2011 to 10 percent of these Federal Reserve System expenses (or approximately $498 million),
- In fiscal year 2012 to 11 percent of these expenses (or approximately $547.8 million),
- In fiscal year 2013 to 12 percent of these expenses (or approximately $597.6 million), and
- In fiscal year 2014 and beyond, the cap remains at 12 percent but will be adjusted for inflation.

The Dodd-Frank Act requires the CFPB to maintain an account with the Federal Reserve – “Bureau of Consumer Financial Protection Fund” (Bureau Fund). Funds requested from the Board of Governors are transferred into the Bureau Fund.

Bureau funds determined not to be needed to meet the current needs of the CFPB are invested in Treasury securities on the open market. Earnings from the investments are also deposited into this fund. During fiscal year 2011, five transfers totaling $161.8 million were received from the Board of Governors[5].

The Dodd-Frank Act explicitly provides that Bureau funds obtained by or transferred to the CFPB are not Government funds or appropriated funds.

The CFPB also collects filing fees from developers as part of the process regarding Interstate Land Settlements (ILS).

The ILS program protects consumers from fraud and abuse in the sale or lease of land. In 1968, Congress enacted the Interstate Land Sales Full Disclosure Act, which is patterned after the Securities Law of 1933 and requires land developers to register subdivisions of 100 or more non-exempt lots and to provide each purchaser with a disclosure document called a Property Report. The Property Report contains relevant information about the subdivision and must be delivered to each purchaser before the signing of the contract or agreement.

On July 21, 2010, this program was transferred to the CFPB from the Department of Housing and Urban Development pursuant the Dodd-Frank Act. While CFPB continues to study the legal effects of the legislation with respect to the transfer of these functions under the Land Sales Act, and the collection of fees, the fees are currently being deposited into an account maintained by Treasury.

The fees collected may be retained and are available until expended for the purpose of covering all or part of the costs that the Bureau incurs for ILS program operations.

Pursuant to the Dodd-Frank Act, the CFPB is also authorized to collect civil penalties against any person in any judicial or administrative action under Federal consumer financial laws.

The Act also requires the CFPB to maintain a separate fund, known as the Consumer Financial Civil Penalty Fund (Civil Penalty Fund). Collections of civil penalties will be deposited into the Civil Penalty Fund, which is in the process of being established. CFPB did not collect any civil penalties during fiscal year 2011.

***What the CFPB has Funded***

During fiscal year 2011, the CFPB was still growing; therefore, the majority of its obligations related to resources essential to standing up the CFPB, such as personnel, information technology, mission-specific and human capital support, and other general start-up activities. The CFPB incurred $123.3 million in obligations – $68.7 million in Contracts & Support Services, $48.4 million in Salary & Benefits, and $6.2 million in All Other – as displayed in the chart to the left:

Some of the larger funded items for the CFPB start-up activities included in the $68.7 million for Contracts and Support Services include:

- $18.6 million to the Department of the Treasury for various services such as, information and technology and human resource systems support and detailees,
- $6 million to the Bureau of the Public Debt for cross-servicing of various human resource and financial management services, such as core financial accounting, transaction processing, travel and payroll,
- $4.4 million to a contractor for human resource policies and assistance in developing salary and benefits packages consistent with the requirements of the Dodd-Frank Act, and,
- $4.3 million to a contractor for the development and maintenance of a Consumer Complaint System.

*Net Costs of the CFPB's Operations*

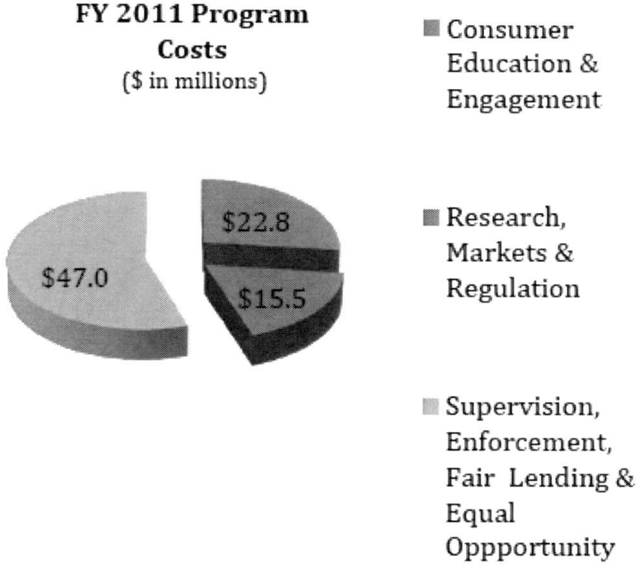


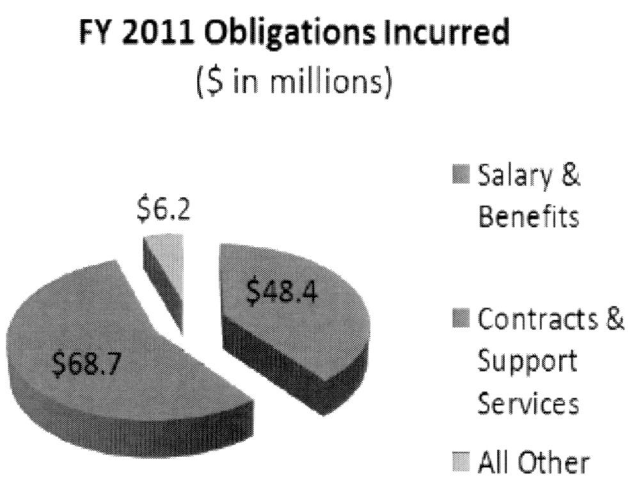


The Statement of Net Cost presents the CFPB gross and net cost for its three strategic missions: Consumer Education & Engagement; Research, Markets & Regulation; and, Supervision, Enforcement, Fair Lending & Equal Opportunity. Total CFPB net costs for fiscal year 2011 in these three programmatic categories are $85.3 million – $47 million for Supervision &

Enforcement, Fair Lending and Equal Opportunity, $22.8 million for Consumer Education and Engagement, and $15.5 million for Research, Markets & Regulation – as displayed in the chart to the left. The majority of costs were incurred in Supervision and Enforcement, Fair Lending and Equal Opportunity including the start-up costs of the program and the majority of CFPB's personnel costs – 51.9% of all hires by year-end.

## VII. Possible Future Risks and Uncertainties

***Potential Funding Concerns and Potential Impact to Independence***

The Dodd-Frank Act followed a long-established precedent in providing the CFPB with funding outside of the Congressional appropriations process. Congress has consistently provided for independent funding for bank supervisors to allow for long-term planning and the execution of complex initiatives and to ensure that banks are examined regularly and thoroughly for both safety and soundness and compliance with the law.

The CFPB has been tasked with supervising more entities than all other federal bank supervisors combined, including supervising the largest, most complex banks. Effective supervision that levels the playing field between bank and non-bank institutions will require dedicated and predictable resources, and independent examiners.

Moreover, consumer compliance examinations for depository institutions with less than $10 billion in assets will continue to be conducted by prudential regulators and thus funded independently. Thus, consumer compliance examinations of community banks and large bank and non-bank institutions will all be funded independently.

Although Congress provided the CFPB with a source of funding outside the appropriations process, the CFPB is nonetheless the only bank supervisor with a statutory cap on its primary source of funding. If the Director were to determine that the non-appropriated funds to which it is entitled under the Act are insufficient to carry out its responsibilities, the Act provides the potential for CFPB to also obtain appropriated funds, up to a capped amount, in fiscal years 2011-2014.

In accordance with the Act and appropriations law requirements, further action would be required on the part of the Director and Congress in order for CFPB to obtain such appropriated funds.

# PART B. FINANCIAL STATEMENTS AND NOTE DISCLOSURES

## Message from the Chief Financial Officer

During fiscal year 2011, the Office of the Chief Financial Officer played a major role in the growth and development of the Consumer Financial Protection Bureau (CFPB).

The CFPB was established by the Dodd-Frank Act when it was enacted on July 21, 2010. Much of the work to establish CFPB as a new bureau occurred during fiscal year 2011.

During this time, the agency grew from 58 employees in the first quarter to 663 employees at fiscal year-end. The rapid growth in employees and the associated offices required a significant level of effort to establish the necessary support structure of the agency.

Some of the CFPB activities the Office of the Chief Financial Officer supported in fiscal year 2011 include:

- Entered into Inter-agency Agreements with other federal agencies to obtain services in the areas of financial management, human resource, procurement, travel, and payroll;
- Designed and developed CFPB's budget and internal control functions;
- Developed CFPB's operating plans;
- Prepared five fund request transfers from the Federal Reserve System totaling $161.8 million; and,
- Coordinated benefits payments for transferees.

As a new stand-up bureau, we recognize that much work remains to be done in fiscal year 2012.

We will continue to work towards strengthening the Office of the Chief Financial Officer and continue to ensure we have sound fiscal policies and a strong internal control environment in place.

I am pleased to present the CFPB's first set of financial statements as an integral part of the fiscal year 2011 Financial Report.

For fiscal year 2011, the Government Accountability Office rendered an unqualified audit opinion on CFPB's financial statements and noted no material weaknesses or significant deficiencies in CFPB's internal controls and cited no instances of non-compliance with laws and regulations.

Stephen Agostini
Chief Financial Officer
Consumer Financial Protection Bureau

Freddy Vélez
Acting Deputy Chief Financial Officer
Consumer Financial Protection Bureau

**Consumer Financial Protection Bureau**
**Balance Sheet**
**As of September 30, 2011**
**(In Dollars)**

| | **2011** |
|---|---|
| **Assets:** | |
| Intragovernmental | |
| Fund Balance with Treasury (Note 2) | $ 18,673,308 |
| Investments (Note 3) | 80,298,806 |
| **Total Intragovernmental** | 98,972,114 |
| Cash, and Other Monetary Assets (Note 4) | 332,021 |
| Accounts Receivable | 7,068 |
| Property, Equipment, and Software, Net (Note 5) | 1,770,214 |
| Advances and Prepayments (Note 6) | 14,689,107 |
| Total Assets | $ 115,770,524 |
| **Liabilities:** | |
| Intragovernmental | |
| Accounts Payable | $ 3,288,536 |
| Other (Note 7) | 1,151,377 |
| **Total Intragovernmental** | 4,439,913 |
| Accounts Payable | 5,728,159 |
| Other (Note 7) | 9,129,788 |
| **Total Liabilities** | $ 19,297,860 |
| **Net Position:** | |
| Cumulative Results of Operations - Earmarked Funds | $ 96,472,664 |
| Total Net Position | $ 96,472,664 |
| Total Liabilities and Net Position | $ 115,770,524 |

## Consumer Financial Protection Bureau Statement of Net Cost For the Fiscal Year Ended September 30, 2011 (In Dollars)

| | 2011 |
|---|---|
| **Program Costs:** | |
| Consumer Education and Engagement (Including Response Center): | |
| Gross Costs | $ 22,831,638 |
| Less: Earned Revenue | - |
| Net Consumer Education and Engagement (Including Response Center) | $ 22,831,638 |
| Research, Markets, and Regulations: | |
| Gross Costs | $ 15,485,938 |
| Less: Earned Revenue | - |
| Net Research, Markets, and Regulations | $ 15,485,938 |
| Supervision, Enforcement, Fair Lending and Equal Opportunity: | |
| Gross Costs | $ 47,011,018 |
| Less: Earned Revenue | - |
| Net Supervision, Enforcement, Fair Lending and Equal Opportunity | $ 47,011,018 |
| Total Gross Program Costs | $ 85,328,594 |
| Less: Total Earned Revenues | - |
| Net Cost of Operations (Note 10) | $ 85,328,594 |

The accompanying notes are an integral part of these financial statements.

## Consumer Financial Protection Bureau Statement of Budgetary Resources For the Fiscal Year Ended September 30, 2011 (In Dollars)

| | 2011 |
|---|---|
| **Budgetary Resources:** | |
| Unobligated Balance Brought Forward, October 1 (Note 11) | $ 9,200,000 |
| Funds Available for Obligation | 161,849,662 |
| 161,849,662 | $ 171,049,662 |
| **Status of Budgetary Resources:** | |
| Obligations Incurred (Note 12) Direct | $ 123,329,760 |
| Unobligated Balance | |
| Exempt From Apportionment | 47,719,902 |
| Total Status of Budgetary Resources | $ 171,049,662 |
| **Change in Obligated Balance:** | |
| Obligated Balance, Net | |
| Unpaid Obligations, Brought Forward, October 1 (Note 11) | $ 9,200,000 |
| Total Unpaid Obligated Balance, Net | $ 9,200,000 |
| Obligations Incurred Net | 123,329,760 |
| Gross Outlays | |
| Obligated Balance, Net, End of Period | |
| Unpaid Obligations | 51,583,044 |
| Total Unpaid Obligated Balance, Net, End of Period | $ 51,583,044 |
| **Net Outlays:** | |
| Gross Outlays | $ 80,946,716 |
| Net Outlays | $ 80,946,716 |

## Note 1. Summary of Significant Accounting Policies

### *A. Reporting Entity*

The Bureau of Consumer Financial Protection, known as the Consumer Financial Protection Bureau (CFPB), was established under the Dodd-Frank Wall Street Reform and Consumer Protection Act P.L.111-203 (Dodd-Frank Act) on July 21, 2010. CFPB was established as an independent bureau within the Federal Reserve System. The Bureau is an Executive agency as defined in section 105 of Title 5, United States Code.

The Dodd-Frank Act authorizes the CFPB to exercise its authorities to ensure that, with respect to consumer financial products and services:

a) Consumers are provided with timely and understandable information to make responsible decisions about financial transactions;
b) Consumers are protected from unfair, deceptive, or abusive acts and practices and from discrimination;
c) Outdated, unnecessary, or unduly burdensome regulations are regularly identified and addressed in order to reduce unwarranted regulatory burdens;
d) Federal consumer financial law is enforced consistently in order to promote fair competition; and
e) Markets for consumer financial products and services operate transparently and efficiently to facilitate access and innovation.

Under the Dodd-Frank Act, on the designated transfer date, July 21, 2011, certain authorities and functions of several agencies relating to Federal consumer financial law were transferred to the CFPB in order to accomplish the above objectives.

These authorities were transferred from the Board of Governors of the Federal Reserve System (Board of Governors), Comptroller of the Currency (OCC), Office of Thrift Supervision (OTS), Federal Deposit Insurance Corporation (FDIC), Federal Trade Commission (FTC), National Credit Union Administration (NCUA), and the Department of Housing and Urban Development (HUD). In addition to these transferred authorities, the Dodd-Frank Act provided the CFPB with certain newly established federal consumer financial regulatory authorities.

To accomplish its mission, the CFPB is organized into six primary divisions/offices:

1. Consumer Education and Engagement

Provides, through a variety of initiatives and methods, information to consumers that will allow them to make decisions that are best for them. Consumer education is a central mission to the Bureau. The Bureau is developing targeted outreach to groups that face particular challenges, as required by the Dodd-Frank Act.

2. Supervision, Enforcement, Fair Lending and Equal Opportunity

Ensures compliance with federal consumer financial laws by supervising market participants and bringing enforcement actions when appropriate.

3. Research, Markets, and Regulations

Responsible for understanding consumer financial markets and consumer behavior, for evaluating whether there is a need for regulation, and for determining the costs and benefits of potential or existing regulations. Before the Bureau acts, it will seek to be fully informed. The offices within this division are staffed with professionals selected for their strong analytic skills and subject matter expertise.

4. Office of General Counsel

Responsible for the Bureau's compliance with all applicable laws and provides advice to the Director and the Bureau's divisions.

5. External Affairs

Ensures that the Bureau maintains robust dialogue with various stakeholders that have an interest in its work in order to promote understanding, transparency, and accountability.

6. Office of Chief Operating Officer

Builds and sustains the CFPB's operational infrastructure to support the entire organization.

The CFPB workforce is spread across the country with its headquarters in Washington, D.C. and regional satellite offices in Chicago, New York City, and San Francisco. The headquarters is temporarily spread across several locations within Washington, D.C., utilizing space rented through interagency agreements with the Department of the Treasury (Treasury). CFPB will eventually consolidate its headquarters into one building in Washington, D.C.

The workforce in CFPB's regional offices is predominantly mobile and therefore minimal office and conference room space is used in the regions.

Additional information on the organizational structure and responsibilities of CFPB is available on CFPB's website at http://www.consumerfinance.gov/.

Under the Dodd-Frank Act, the Secretary of the Treasury is responsible for establishing the CFPB and exercising certain of its authorities until a Director of the CFPB is in place. On July 18, 2011 President Obama sent to the Senate a nomination for a Director of CFPB. The CFPB is still without a Director and continues to operate under the authority of the Secretary of the Treasury. The Bureau's day-to-day operations are managed by the Special Advisor to the Secretary of the Treasury for the Consumer Financial Protection Bureau.

### *B. Basis of Presentation*

CFPB's principal statements were prepared from its official financial records and general ledger in conformity with accounting principles generally accepted in the United States and follows the general presentation guidance established by OMB Circular A-136, *Financial Reporting Requirements,* as revised. The financial statements are a requirement of the Dodd-Frank Act. The financial statements are in addition to the financial reports prepared by CFPB, pursuant to OMB directives, which are used to monitor and control budgetary resources. The financial statements have been prepared to report the financial position, net cost of operations, changes in net position, and the status and availability of budgetary resources of CFPB. The financial statements and associated notes are presented on a single year basis. This is the first full year of operation for the CFPB and therefore comparative statements are not presented.

The net cost of operations is presented by the three primary objectives of the Bureau – educate, enforce, and study – and is consistent with CFPB's organizational structure.

### *C. Basis of Accounting*

Transactions are recorded on both an accrual accounting basis and a budgetary basis. Under the accrual basis of accounting, revenues are recognized when earned, and expenses are recognized when a liability is incurred, without regard to receipt or payment of cash. Budgetary accounting facilitates compliance with legal requirements and controls over the use of federal funds. CFPB conforms to accounting principles generally accepted in the United States for federal entities as prescribed by the standards set forth by the Federal Accounting Standards Advisory Board (FASAB). FASAB is recognized by the American Institute of Certified Public Accountants as the body designated to establish generally accepted accounting principles for federal government entities. Certain assets, liabilities, earned revenues, and costs have been classified as intragovernmental throughout the financial statements and notes. Intragovernmental assets and liabilities are those due from or to other federal entities. Intragovernmental earned revenues are collections or accruals due from other federal entities. Intragovernmental costs are payments or accruals due to other federal entities.

CFPB has rights and ownership of all assets reported in these financial statements. CFPB does not possess any non-entity assets.

***D. Funding Sources***

Funding needed for carrying out the mission of CFPB is obtained primarily through transfers from the Board of Governors, interest earned on investments, and penalties and fees collected. The Dodd-Frank Act requires the CFPB to maintain an account with the Federal Reserve – "Bureau of Consumer Financial Protection Fund" (Bureau Fund). The Director of CFPB, or designee, requests transfers from the Board of Governors in amounts necessary to carry out the authorities and operations of the Bureau. The Board of Governors transfers the funds into the Bureau Fund, which is maintained at the Federal Reserve Bank of New York (FRBNY). Bureau funds determined not needed to meet the current needs of the Bureau are invested in Treasury securities on the open market. Earnings from the investments are also deposited into this fund. Going forward, CFPB anticipates requesting funds on a quarterly basis. The funds maintained by the FRBNY are reported in the financial statements and related notes and represent budget authority for CFPB.

The CFPB funding requests for the Bureau Fund are capped as follows:

The amount that shall be transferred to the Bureau in each fiscal year shall not exceed a fixed percentage of the total operating expenses of the Federal Reserve System, subject to an annual inflation adjustment, as reported in the Annual Report, 2009, of the Board of Governors, equal to:

1) 10 percent of such expenses in fiscal year 2011,
2) 11 percent of such expenses in fiscal year 2012,
3) 12 percent of such expenses in fiscal year 2013, and in each year thereafter.

The Dodd-Frank Act explicitly provides that Bureau funds obtained by or transferred to CFPB are not Government funds or appropriated funds.

If the Director were to determine that the non-appropriated funds to which it is entitled under the Act are insufficient to carry out its responsibilities, the Act provides the potential for CFPB to also obtain appropriated funds, up to a capped amount, in fiscal years 2011-2014. In accordance with the Act and appropriations law requirements, further action would be required on the part of the Director and Congress in order for CFPB to obtain such appropriated funds.

The CFPB also collects filing fees from developers as part of the process regarding Interstate Land Settlements (ILS). The Interstate Land Settlements program protects consumers from fraud and abuse in the sale or lease of land. In 1968 Congress enacted the Interstate Land Sales Full Disclosure Act, which is patterned after the Securities Law of 1933 and requires land developers to register subdivisions of 100 or more non-exempt lots and to provide each purchaser with a disclosure document called a Property Report. The Property Report contains relevant information about the subdivision and must be delivered to each purchaser before the signing of the contract or agreement. On July 21, 2011, this program was transferred to the CFPB from HUD pursuant the Dodd-Frank Act. While CFPB continues to study the legal effects of the legislation with respect to the transfer of these functions under the Land Sales Act, and the collection of fees, the fees are currently being deposited into an account maintained by Treasury. The fees collected may be retained and are available until expended for the purpose of covering all or part of the costs that the Bureau incurs for ILS program operations.

Pursuant to the Dodd-Frank Act, the CFPB is also authorized to collect civil penalties against any person in any judicial or administrative action under Federal consumer financial laws. The Act also requires the CFPB to maintain a separate fund, known as the Consumer Financial Civil Penalty Fund (Civil Penalty Fund).

Collections of civil penalties will be deposited into the Civil Penalty Fund, which will be maintained by the FRBNY. The Civil Penalty Fund is in the process of being established. CFPB did not collect any civil penalties for fiscal year 2011.

CFPB also recognizes imputed financing sources. An imputed financing source is recognized by the receiving entity for costs that are paid by other entities. CFPB recognized imputed costs and financing sources in fiscal year 2011 as prescribed by accounting standards. CFPB recognizes as an imputed financing source the amount of pension expenses for OCC and the Office of

Personnel Management (OPM) and post-retirement benefit expenses for OPM for current employees accrued on CFPB's behalf.

### *E. Use of Estimates*

The Bureau has made certain estimates and assumptions relating to the reporting of assets, liabilities, revenues, expenses, and the disclosure of contingent liabilities to prepare these financial statements. Actual results could differ from these estimates. Significant transactions subject to estimates include costs regarding benefit plans for CFPB employees that are administered by the OPM, OCC, FDIC, and the Federal Reserve System and cost allocations among the programs on the Statement of Net Cost.

### *F. Earmarked Funds*

FASAB's Statement of Federal Financial Accounting Standards (SFFAS) No. 27 *Identifying and Reporting Earmarked Funds* established certain disclosure requirements for funds defined as "earmarked." SFFAS No. 27 states that "earmarked funds are financed by specifically identified revenues, often supplemented by other financing sources, which remain available over time. These specifically identified revenues and other financing sources are required by statute to be used for designated activities, benefits or purposes and must be accounted for separately from the Government's general revenues." The standard also presents three required criteria for an earmarked fund. Based on the standard's criteria, CFPB is an earmarked fund due to its primary funding sources being transfers from the Board of Governors, interest on investments, and fees from the ILS program.

### *G. Fund Balance with Treasury*

The U.S. Treasury holds funds in the Treasury General Account for CFPB which are available to pay agency liabilities and finance authorized purchase obligations. Treasury processes cash receipts and disbursements on CFPB's behalf, such as fees collected from the ILS program. As discussed in Note 1.D. above, CFPB also maintains an account with the FRBNY known as the Bureau Fund. During the year, increases to the Bureau Fund are generally comprised of fund transfers from the Board of Governors and investment interest. These funds are available for transfer to CFPB's Fund balance with Treasury. CFPB's Fund Balance with Treasury is maintained in a special fund. A special fund is established where the law requires collections to be earmarked from a specified source to finance a particular program, and the law neither authorizes the fund to conduct a cycle of business-type operations (making it a revolving fund) nor designates it as a trust fund.

### *H. Investments*

CFPB has the authority to invest the funds in the Bureau Fund account that are not required to meet the current needs of the Bureau. CFPB invests solely in U.S. Treasury securities purchased at a discount on the open market, which are normally held to maturity and carried at cost. CFPB selects investments with maturities suitable to its needs, currently three month Treasury bills. Investments are adjusted for discounts. In accordance with generally accepted accounting principles, the CFPB records the value of its investments in U.S. Treasury securities at cost and amortizes the discount on a straight-line basis over the term of the respective issues. Interest is credited to the Bureau Fund.

### *I. Accounts Receivable*

Accounts receivable consists of amounts owed to CFPB by the public. An allowance for uncollectible accounts receivable from the public is established when either (1) management determines that collection is unlikely to occur after a review of outstanding accounts and the failure of all collection efforts, or (2) an account for which no allowance has been established is submitted to Treasury for collection, which takes place when it becomes 180 days delinquent.

### *J. Property, Equipment, and Software, Net*

Property, Equipment, and Software is recorded at historical cost. It consists of tangible assets and software. Under CFPB's property management policy equipment acquisitions of $50 thousand or more are capitalized and depreciated using the straight-line method over the estimated useful life of the asset. Similarly, internal use software, software purchased or developed to facilitate the operation of an entity's programs, is capitalized for software of $750 thousand or more and depreciated using the straight-line method over the estimated useful life of the asset. Additionally, for bulk purchases of similar items, which individually do not meet the test to capitalize, the acquisition is capitalized and depreciated if the depreciated basis of the bulk purchase is $250 thousand or more. Applicable standard governmental guidelines regulate the disposal and convertibility of agency property and equipment. The useful life classifications for capitalized assets are as follows:

| PP&E Category | Useful Lives (years) |
|---|---|
| Laptop/Desktop Computers | 3 |
| Internal Use Software | 5 |
| Mainframe Computer System | 7 |
| Servers | 7 |
| Telecommunications Equipment | 7 |
| Furniture | 8 |
| Other Equipment | 10 |

A leasehold improvement's useful life is equal to the remaining lease term or the estimated useful life of the improvement, whichever is shorter. CFPB has no real property holdings or stewardship or heritage assets. Other property items, normal repairs and maintenance are charged to expense as incurred.

***K. Advances and Prepaid Charges***

Advances and prepayments may occur as a result of reimbursable agreements, subscriptions, payments to contractors and employees, and payments to entities administering benefit programs for CFPB employees. Payments made in advance of the receipt of goods and services are recorded as advances or prepaid charges at the time of prepayment and recognized as expenses when the related goods and services are received.

***L. Liabilities***

Liabilities represent the amount of monies likely to be paid by CFPB as a result of transactions or events that have already occurred. Liabilities may be intragovernmental (claims against the CFPB by other Federal agencies) or with the public (claims against CFPB by an entity or person that is not a Federal agency). However, no liability can be paid if there is no funding. Liabilities for which funds are not available, therefore, are classified as not covered by budgetary resources. There is no certainty that the funding will be received. Additionally, the Government, acting in its sovereign capacity, can abrogate liabilities. Liabilities not covered by budgetary resources on the Balance Sheet are equivalent to amounts reported as components not requiring or generating resources on the Reconciliation of Net Cost to Budget.

***M. Annual, Sick, and Other Leave***

Annual leave and credit hours earned by the Bureau's employees, but not yet used, are reported as accrued liabilities. The accrued balance is adjusted annually to current pay rates. The accrued leave, for which funding is not available, is recorded as an unfunded liability. Sick and other leave are expensed as taken.

***N. Employee Benefits***

CFPB employees are enrolled in various benefit programs – medical, vision, dental, long-term disability, and life insurance. Employees also have options regarding which benefit programs to enroll.

**Benefits for Employees Transferred Pursuant to the Dodd-Frank Act**

The Dodd-Frank Act provided employees transferred from other agencies (Board of Governors, Federal Reserve Banks, OCC, OTS, FDIC, NCUA, and HUD) with the ability to continue participation in some of the transferring agencies' non-Title 5 benefit programs for a defined amount of time (one year from the CFPB transfer date of July 21, 2011). Title 5 of the U.S. Code outlines benefit programs for the majority of the Federal workforce, in which the programs are typically administered by OPM. The transferring agencies continue to administer the non-Title 5 benefit programs for those transferred employees. Upon conclusion of the defined period of time, the employees may enroll in non-Title 5 benefit programs sponsored by CFPB. For those employees participating in the transferring agencies' programs, CFPB reimburses the transferring agencies for the employer's contribution to the programs. CFPB may also reimburse the transferring agencies for administrative costs pursuant to memoranda of understanding with the transferring agencies. These costs are reflected as expenses in CFPB's financial statements.

**Benefits for Employees Not Transferred Pursuant to the Dodd-Frank Act**

Employees not transferred to the Bureau pursuant to the Dodd-Frank Act are enrolled in benefit programs administered by OPM and also have the option to enroll in non-Title 5 benefit programs sponsored by CFPB in addition to, or in lieu of, OPM programs. For those employees participating in OPM's benefit programs, CFPB records the employer's contribution to those programs. OPM records the liability and pays for these programs on behalf of all of the Federal agencies participating in the programs. For those employees participating in CFPB's non-Title 5 benefit programs, CFPB directly contracts with vendors to provide those services. The Bureau recognizes the employer's contributions for these benefits as the benefits are earned. All of these costs are reflected as expenses in CFPB's financial statements.

### *O. Pension Costs and Other Retirement Benefits*

CFPB employees are enrolled in several retirement and pension programs and post-employment benefits in accordance with the authorities in the Dodd-Frank Act.

### Employees Transferred from the Federal Reserve, OCC, OTS, FDIC, and HUD

The Dodd-Frank Act allowed employees transferred from OCC, OTS, FDIC, and HUD, under the terms of the Act, to continue participating in the pension or retirement plans in which they were enrolled at their transferring agency or to affirmatively elect, from January 21, 2012 to January 20, 2013, to join the Federal Reserve System Retirement Plan and the Federal Reserve System Thrift Plan. Many transferee employees from these agencies are in the traditional Title 5 retirement plans (Federal Employee Retirement System (FERS), Civil Service Retirement System (CSRS), or CSRS Offset); however, a few transferees from OTS are in a non-Title 5 plan (i.e., Pentegra Defined Benefit Plan). Transferees from the Federal Reserve are allowed to remain in the Federal Reserve System retirement program or to affirmatively elect into the appropriate Title 5 retirement plan during that same timeframe. For those employees electing to enroll in an alternative retirement plan, the enrollment will become effective in January 2013.

CFPB does not report on its financial statements information pertaining to the retirement plans covering its employees. Reporting amounts such as plan assets, accumulated plan benefits, and related unfunded liabilities, if any, is the responsibility of the Federal Reserve System, OCC, or OPM as the administrator of their respective plans. In all cases, CFPB pays any employer contributions required by the plans. Refer to the chart below for information on which agency administers each of the retirement plans for CFPB employees.

OCC, OTS, and FDIC also offered other agency-only savings plans to employees. Any transferees who participated in such plans are allowed to continue their participation as long as they remain enrolled in their current retirement plans. In such cases, CFPB pays any employer contributions. Employees who elect to enroll in the Federal Reserve retirement plan will not be allowed to continue their participation in either the Title 5 Thrift Savings Plan or OCC, OTS, and FDIC agency savings plans.

CFPB may also reimburse the transferring agencies for administrative costs pursuant to memoranda of understanding with the transferring agencies. These costs are reflected as expenses in CFPB's financial statements.

## All Other Employees of CFPB

Employees hired with prior Title 5 Federal Retirement System coverage who are not transferees under the Dodd Frank Act are enrolled in the appropriate retirement programs administered by OPM – CSRS, CSRS Offset, or FERS. These employees also have the option, within one year of appointment, to enroll in the Federal Reserve System retirement plans. CFPB will begin providing employees the opportunity to enroll in the Federal Reserve retirement system plans beginning in November 2011. For those employees electing to enroll in the Federal Reserve System retirement plans, the enrollment will become effective at the beginning of the pay period following receipt of their written election decision. Employees that were hired from the private sector, with no previous coverage under a Title 5 retirement plan, are automatically enrolled in the Federal Reserve System's retirement plans. CFPB pays the employer's contribution into those plans.

## Pension/Retirement Plans for CFPB Employees

| Name | Administering Agency |
|---|---|
| Federal Reserve System Retirement Plan | Federal Reserve System |
| Federal Reserve System Thrift Plan | Federal Reserve System |
| Pension Enhancement Plan for Officers of the Board of Governors of the Federal Reserve System[1] | Federal Reserve System |
| Retirement Plan for Employees of the Federal Reserve System Benefits Equalization Plan[1] | Federal Reserve System |
| Retirement Plan for Employees of the Federal Reserve System Benefits Equalization Plan for Section 415 Excess Benefits[1] | Federal Reserve System |
| Thrift Plan for Employees of the Federal Reserve System Benefits Equalization Plan[1] | Federal Reserve System |
| Civil Service Retirement System (CSRS) | OPM |
| CSRS Offset | OPM |
| Federal Employees' Retirement System (FERS) | OPM |
| Thrift Savings Plan | Federal Retirement Thrift Investment Board |
| FDIC Savings Plan | FDIC |
| OCC 401(k) | OCC |
| OTS 401(k) | OCC |
| OTS Deferred Compensation Plan | OCC |
| Pentegra Defined Benefit Plan (OTS) | OCC (administration is through Pentegra) |

[1] This retirement program does not have any CFPB participants for fiscal year 2011.

The Bureau does not have a separate pension or retirement plan distinct from the plans described above. CFPB expenses its contributions to the retirement plans of covered employees as the expenses are incurred. CFPB reported imputed (unfunded) costs with respect to retirement plans (OPM and OCC administered), health benefits and life insurance (OPM administered) pursuant to guidance received from OPM and OCC. These costs are paid by OPM and OCC and not by CFPB. Disclosure is intended to provide information regarding the full cost of CFPB's program in conformity with generally accepted accounting principles.

The Bureau recognizes the employer's contributions for the retirement plans administered by the Federal Reserve. The Bureau however is responsible for transferring the employer's and employee's contributions to the Federal Reserve. The FRBNY records the full costs and liability and pays for the retirement plans on behalf of the Federal Reserve System and CFPB.

***P. Commitments and Contingencies***

A commitment is a preliminary action that will ultimately result in an obligation to the U.S. government if carried through, such as purchase requisitions or unsigned contracts.

A contingency is an existing condition, situation, or set of circumstances involving uncertainty as to possible gain or loss to an entity that will ultimately be resolved when one or more future confirming events occur or fail to occur. The future confirming event or events are more likely than not to occur, with the exception of pending or threatened litigation and unasserted claims. For pending or threatened litigation and unasserted claims, the future confirming event or events are likely to occur. In accordance with Statement of Federal Financial Accounting Standards No. 5, *Accounting for Liabilities of the Federal Government*, contingent future outflows or other sacrifices of resources as a result of past transactions or events may be recognized, may be disclosed, or may not be reported at all, depending on the circumstances. Contingencies should be recognized as a liability when a past transaction or event has occurred, a future outflow or other sacrifice of resources is probable, and the related future outflow or sacrifice of resources is measurable. A contingent liability should be disclosed if any of the conditions for liability recognition are not met and there is a reasonable possibility that a loss or an additional loss may have been incurred. Disclosure should include the nature of the contingency and an estimate of the possible liability, an estimate of the range of the possible liability, or a statement that such an estimate cannot be made.

## Note 2. Fund Balance with Treasury

Fund Balance with Treasury account balances as of September 30, 2011, were as follows:

| (In Dollars) | **2011** |
|---|---|
| **Fund Balance:** | |
| Special Fund | $ 18,673,308 |
| Total | $ 18,673,308 |
| **Status of Fund Balance with Treasury:** | |
| Unobligated Balance | |
| Available | $ 47,719,902 |
| Unavailable | - |
| Obligated Balance Not Yet Disbursed | 51,583,044 |
| Investments (at Cost) (See Note 3) | (80,297,617) |
| Cash Held in the Bureau Fund at the Federal Reserve | (332,021) |
| (See Note 4) | |
| Total | $ 18,673,308 |

Unobligated Balance Available represents the amount of budget authority that can be used to enter into new obligations. This amount, or a portion thereof, may be administratively dedicated for specific purposes that have not yet been obligated. The Obligated Balance Not Yet Disbursed represents amounts designated for payment of goods and services ordered but not received or goods and services received but for which payment has not yet been made.

## Note 3. Investments

As discussed further in Note 4, the Board of Governors at the discretion of the CFPB can invest the portion of the Bureau Fund that is not, in the judgment of the Bureau, required to meet the current needs of the Bureau. When directed by CFPB, the FRBNY will utilize the funds available to purchase investments on the open market. CFPB only invests in three month U.S. Treasury bills. The market value is determined by the secondary U.S. Treasury market and represents the value an individual investor is willing to pay for these securities, as of September 30, 2011.

Investments as of September 30, 2011 consist of the following:

| (In Dollars) | Cost | Amortization Method | Amortized (Premium) Discount | Investments Net | Market Value Disclosure |
|---|---|---|---|---|---|
| **Intragovernmental Securities:** | | | | | |
| Marketable | $80,297,617 | Straight-Line | $ 1,189 | $ 80,298,806 | $ 80,297,603 |
| Total | $80,297,617 | | $ 1,189 | $ 80,298,806 | $ 80,297,603 |

## Note 4. Cash and Other Monetary Assets

CFPB has both cash and investments held outside of Treasury. When transfers are made from the Board of Governors to CFPB, the funds are deposited into an account held within the FRBNY referred to as the Bureau Fund. The account has a required minimum balance of $250,000 and any funds in excess of this minimum are invested in Treasury securities in increments of $100,000 by the FRBNY utilizing an automatic investment process. CFPB requests cash disbursement from the Bureau Fund to the CFPB's Fund Balance with Treasury based on projections of future expenditures.

Funds obtained by, transferred to, or credited to the Bureau Fund are immediately available to CFPB and under the control of the Director, and shall remain available until expended, to pay for the expenses of the Bureau in carrying out its duties and responsibilities. Funds obtained by or transferred to the Bureau Fund shall not be construed to be Government funds or appropriated monies. These funds are not subject to apportionment for purposes of chapter 15 Title 31, United States Code, or under any other authority.

Account balance as of September 30, 2011:

| (In Dollars) | 2011 |
|---|---|
| **Cash** | |
| Cash Held in the Bureau Fund at the Federal Reserve | $ 332,021 |
| Total Cash and Other Monetary Assets | $ 332,021 |

## Note 5. Property, Equipment and Software, Net

Schedule of Property, Equipment, and Software as of September 30, 2011:

| **Major Class** ( *In Dollars*) | **Acquisition Cost** | **Accumulated Amortization/ Depreciation** | **Net Book Value** |
|---|---|---|---|
| Equipment | $ 997,719 | $ 108,490 | $ 889,229 |
| Internal Use Software | 978,872 | 97,887 | 880,985 |
| Total | $ 1,976,591 | $ 206,377 | 1,770,214 |

## Note 6. Advances and Prepayments

Advances and Prepayment balance as of September 30, 2011 were as follows:

| (In Dollars) | **2011** |
|---|---|
| With the Public | |
| Advances and Prepayments | $ 14,689,107 |
| Total Public Advances and Prepayments | $ 14,689,107 |

The prepayment primarily represents a payment of $14.4 million to the Federal Reserve System for the Federal Reserve System retirement plans to cover the time in service for employees transferred to CFPB under Section 1064 of the Dodd-Frank Act who were previously covered by an OPM or OTS retirement plan. Pursuant to Section 1064 of the Dodd-Frank Act, employees transferred to CFPB may enroll in the Federal Reserve System Retirement Plan and Federal Reserve System Thrift Plan. If the transferred employee chooses to enroll in these plans, CFPB has to transfer to the Federal Reserve System Retirement Plan an amount determined by the Board of Governors in consultation with CFPB to reimburse the Federal Reserve System Retirement Plan for the costs of providing the transferred employees' benefits under this plan. The $14.4 million payment was based on a projection of CFPB employees likely to enroll in the Federal Reserve System Retirement Plan. A memorandum of understanding between the Board of Governors and the Bureau established that the Board of Governors would provide the Bureau a final cost estimate for this payment by September 30, 2014. This prepayment represents the amount agreed to by the Board of Governors and Bureau to fund the Federal Reserve Plan Trust until the final cost estimate is complete. The amount is calculated using actuarial assumptions. Other prepayments include subscriptions and other miscellaneous items.

## Note 7. Other Liabilities

Other liabilities as of September 30, 2011 consist of the following:

| (In Dollars) | **Total** |
|---|---|
| Intragovernmental Liabilities | |
| Payroll Taxes Payable | $ 257,336 |
| Benefits Payable | 894,041 |
| Total Intragovernmental Liabilities | $ 1,151,377 |
| With the Public | |
| Employee Withholdings | $ 14,536 |
| Employer Benefits Contributions | 817,293 |
| Accrued Funded Payroll | 817,293 |
| Unfunded Leave | 3,982,285 |
| Total Public Liabilities | $ 9,129,788 |

All other liabilities are considered current liabilities.

## Note 8. Liabilities Not Covered by Budgetary Resources

Liabilities not covered by budgetary resources as of September 30, 2011 consists of unfunded leave of $3,982,285.

## Note 9. Commitments and Contingencies

As described in Note 6, CFPB is responsible for reimbursing the Federal Reserve Retirement Plan for certain costs related to employees, transferred to CFPB under Section 1064 of the Dodd Frank Act, that enroll in the Plan. As described in note 1.O. employees will be given the opportunity to elect to enroll into the Plan from January 21, 2012 to January 20, 2013, therefore the number of employees that will elect to enroll in the Plan is not known as of September 30, 2011. Consequently, a contingent liability and related expense are not recognized as of September 30, 2011, because the amount to be reimbursed is not measurable.

## Note 10. Intragovernmental Costs and Exchange Revenue

Intragovernmental costs and intragovernmental exchange revenue represent goods and services provided between two reporting entities within the Federal government, and are in contrast to those with non-federal entities (the public). Such costs and revenue are summarized as follows:

***By Program***

| (In Dollars) | **2011** |
|---|---|
| Consumer Education and Engagement (Including Response Center) | |
| Intragovernmental Costs | $ 9,947,744 |
| Public Costs | 12,883,894 |
| Total Program Costs | 22,831,638 |
| Net Consumer Education and Engagement Cost | $ 22,831,638 |
| Research, Markets, and Regulations | |
| Intragovernmental Costs | $ 6,747,223 |
| Public Costs | 8,738,715 |
| Total Program Costs | 15,485,938 |
| Net Research, Markets, and Regulations Cost | $ 15,485,938 |
| Supervision, Enforcement, Fair Lending and Equal Opportunity | |
| Intragovernmental Costs | $ 20,482,699 |
| Public Costs | 26,528,319 |
| Total Program Costs | 47,011,018 |
| Net Supervision, Enforcement, Fair Lending and Equal Opportunity Cost | $ 47,011,018 |
| Total Intragovernmental Costs | $ 37,177,666 |
| Total Public Costs | 48,150,928 |
| Total Program Costs | 85,328,594 |
| Less: Total Public Earned Revenue | - |
| Total Program Net Cost | $ 85,328,594 |

## Note 11. Beginning Balances

CFPB was established on July 21, 2010 and had minimal activity in fiscal year 2010, which related primarily to an initial fund transfer received from the Federal Reserve Bank. All amounts are for the period ended September 30, 2010:

| (In Dollars) | **2011** |
|---|---|
| Funds Received from Federal Reserve | $ 18,400,000 |
| Operating Costs | (143,345) |
| Cumulative Results of Operations | $ 18,256,655 |
| Funds Available for Obligation | $ 18,400,000 |
| Obligations Incurred | (9,200,000) |
| Unobligated Balance | $ 9,200,000 |

## Note 12. Apportionment Categories of Obligations Incurred

All obligations incurred are characterized as Category C, Exempt from Apportionment (i.e. not apportioned), on the Statement of Budgetary Resources. Obligations incurred and reported in the Statement of Budgetary Resources in fiscal year 2011 consisted of the following:

| (In Dollars) | **2011** |
|---|---|
| Direct Obligations, Category C | $ 123,329,760 |
| Total Obligations Incurred | $ 123,329,760 |

## Note 13. Undelivered Orders at the End of the Period

Statement of Federal Financial Accounting Standards No. 7, *Accounting for Revenue and Other Financing Sources and Concepts for Reconciling Budgetary and Financial Accounting*, states that the amount of budgetary resources obligated for undelivered orders at the end of the period should be disclosed. CFPB's Undelivered Orders represent obligated amounts designated for payment of goods and services ordered but not received.

Undelivered Orders as of September 30, 2011 were $36,267,469.

## Note 14. Reconciliation of Net Cost to Budget

CFPB has reconciled its budgetary obligations and non-budgetary resources available to its net cost of operations for the year ended September 30, 2011.

| (In Dollars) | **2011** |
|---|---|
| **Resources Used to Finance Activities:** | |
| Budgetary Resources Obligated | |
| Obligations Incurred | $ 123,329,760 |
| Less: Spending Authority From Offsetting Collections and Recoveries | - |
| Less: Offsetting Receipts | - |
| Net Obligations | 123,329,760 |
| Other Resources | |
| Imputed Financing From Costs Absorbed By Others | 1,693,752 |
| Total Resources Used to Finance Activities | 125,023,512 |

| (In Dollars) | **2011** |
|---|---|
| **Resources Used to Finance Items Not Part of the Net Cost of Operations:** | |
| Change In Budgetary Resources Obligated For Goods, Services and Benefits Ordered But Not Yet Provided | (41,899,921) |
| Resources That Finance the Acquisition of Assets | (1,976,591) |
| Total Resources Used to Finance Items Not Part of Net Cost of Operations | (43,876,512) |
| Total Resources Used to Finance the Net Cost of Operations | 81,147,000 |
| **Components of the Net Cost of Operations That Will Not Require or Generate Resources in the Current Period:** | |
| Components Requiring or Generating Resources in Future Periods | |
| Increase In Annual Leave Liability | 3,982,285 |
| Components Not Requiring or Generating Resources | |
| Depreciation and Amortization | 206,377 |
| Other | (7,068) |
| Total Components of Net Cost of Operations That Will Not Require or Generate Resources In The Current Period | 4,181,594 |
| Net Cost of Operations | $ 85,328,594 |

## Note 15. President's Budget

Statement of Federal Financial Accounting Standards No. 7, *Accounting for Revenue and Other Financing Sources and Concepts for Reconciling Budgetary and Financial Accounting*, requires explanations of material differences between amounts reported in the Statement of Budgetary Resources and the actual balances published in the Budget of the United States Government (President's Budget). However, the President's Budget that will include fiscal year 2011 actual budgetary execution information has not yet been published. Therefore the reconciliation of fiscal year 2011 balances will be reported next year since CFPB is a first-year entity.

## End Notes

[1] The Dodd-Frank Act under Section 1064 provides for the transfer of certain employees from the Board of Governors of the Federal Reserve System, Federal Deposit Insurance Corporation,

National Credit Union Administration, Office of the Comptroller of the Currency, Office of Thrift Supervision, and the Department of Housing and Urban Development.

[2] Under the Dodd-Frank Act, the functions and responsibilities for consumer financial protection laws were transferred to the CFPB from seven Federal agencies; however, the Federal Trade Commission was not required to transfer any employees to CFPB per Section 1061 (b) (A).

[3] Under the Dodd-Frank Act, authorities for consumer financial protection were transferred from the Board of Governors of the Federal Reserve System, Comptroller of the Currency, Office of Thrift Supervision, Federal Deposit Insurance Corporation, Federal Trade Commission, National Credit Union Administration, and the Department of Housing and Urban Development.

[4] The CFPB is preparing a strategic plan to help guide its future-years activities beginning in fiscal year 2012.

[5] In fiscal year 2010, one transfer for $18.4 million was received from the Board of Governors.

In: The Consumer Financial Protection Bureau ISBN 978-1-62257-637-1
Editors: P. J. Cerutti and M. Kolchak 

*Chapter 6*

# CONSUMER RESPONSE ANNUAL REPORT*

## *Consumer Financial Protection Bureau*

## MESSAGE FROM RICHARD CORDRAY DIRECTOR OF THE CFPB

On July 21, 2011, the Consumer Financial Protection Bureau ("CFPB" or "Bureau") began consumer response operations as the country's first federal agency specifically mandated to protect American consumers in the financial marketplace. This Consumer Response Report to Congress describes how the Bureau is doing just that.

The CFPB's Consumer Response team started accepting credit card complaints from consumers last year. In December 2011, the Bureau began accepting consumer complaints on mortgages. This year, we have expanded to accept complaints about other bank products and services, private student loans, and a variety of consumer loans. We expect to handle consumer complaints about all products and services within our authority by the end of 2012. Extensive cooperation from our fellow agencies helped ensure that there were no gaps in complaint handling during the rollout of the Bureau's complaint handling capacity.

---

* This is an edited, reformatted and augmented version of Consumer Financial Protection Bureau, dated March 31, 2012.

We provide these services to consumers in 187 languages, and our contact centers answer calls with little-to-no wait time. We are making every effort to be accessible to the American public – from our website's "Tell Your Story" feature, to our toll-free phone number, to our trips across the country to hear from consumers and industry representatives. The input we have received has been exceedingly informative and helped ensure we fulfill our mandate.

This report not only provides an accounting of our consumer response efforts, but also shows that we have been successful in helping consumers resolve disputes with financial services companies. We will continue to meet this challenge and to fulfill Congress's vision that we stand on the side of consumers to help improve their financial lives.

Sincerely,

Richard Cordray

## INTRODUCTION

The Consumer Financial Protection Bureau ("CFPB" or "Bureau") began consumer response operations on July 21, 2011 and became the first federal agency solely focused on consumer financial protection. The Dodd-Frank Wall Street Reform and Consumer Protection Act of 2010 ("Dodd-Frank Act") created the Bureau to protect consumers of financial products or services and to encourage the fair and competitive operation of consumer financial markets. Taking in, resolving, and analyzing consumer complaints[1] is an integral part of the CFPB's work, as Congress set forth in the Dodd-Frank Act.[2] The Bureau's Consumer Response team hears directly from consumers about the challenges they face in the marketplace, brings their concerns to the attention of financial institutions, and assists in addressing their complaints.

The Consumer Response team began taking consumer complaints about credit cards on July 21, 2011; it began handling mortgage complaints on December 1, 2011; and it began accepting complaints about bank products and services, private student loans, and other consumer loans on March 1, 2012.

The CFPB's phased-in approach to taking complaints has allowed Consumer Response to develop strong foundations over time. Based on feedback from consumers and companies, as well as its own observations, the Consumer Response team identifies new opportunities to improve its processes and implement changes with each product launch. By applying the lessons learned through previous complaint function rollouts, the Consumer Response team has improved its intake process, enhanced communication with companies, and ensured the system's ease-of-use and effectiveness for consumers. The CFPB aims to provide services that are trusted by consumers and companies alike and, by the end of 2012, expects to handle consumer complaints on all products and services under its authority.

Consumers may contact the CFPB about products and services beyond those listed above. The Bureau answers these inquiries and refers consumers to other regulators or additional resources where appropriate.

The CFPB also created a "Tell Your Story" feature on its website that gives consumers the opportunity to share their experiences – positive or negative – with consumer financial products and services. These submissions, like formal complaints, are reviewed by CFPB staff to help the Bureau understand current issues in the financial marketplace.

In keeping with the CFPB's statutory responsibility and its commitment to accountability, this report provides an overview of how Consumer Response handles complaints and presents an analysis of complaints received over the period from July 21 through December 31, 2011.[3]

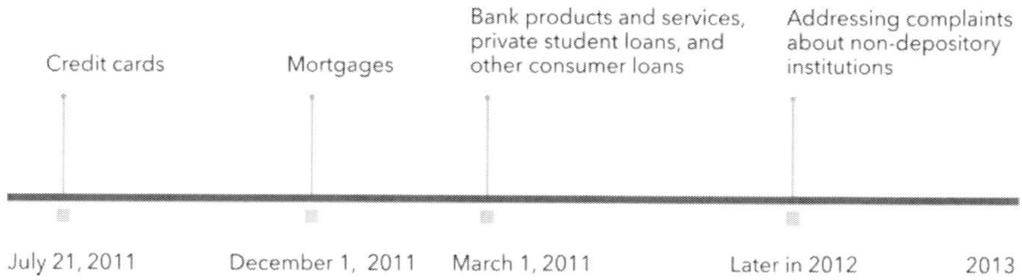


## How The CFPB Handles Complaints

The CFPB accepts complaints through its website and by telephone, mail, email, fax, and referral from other agencies. The CFPB's U.S.-based contact centers handle calls with little-to-no wait times, providing services to consumers in 187 languages and for hearing- and speech-impaired consumers via a toll-free telephone number. Cutting-edge technology, including secure company and consumer portals, makes the process efficient and user-friendly for consumers and companies. For companies, the CFPB provides secure channels for communicating directly with dedicated staff about technical issues.

Consumer Response screens all complaints submitted by consumers based on several criteria. These criteria include whether the complaint falls within the CFPB's primary enforcement authority, whether the complaint is complete, or whether it is a duplicate of a prior submission by the same consumer. Screened complaints are sent via a secure web portal to the appropriate company.[4] The company reviews the information, communicates with the consumer as needed, and determines what action to take in response. The company reports back to the consumer and the CFPB via the secure "company portal." The Bureau then invites the consumer to review the response. Consumer Response prioritizes for review and investigation complaints in which the consumer disputes the response or where companies fail to provide a timely response.[5] Consumers can log onto the secure "consumer portal" available on the CFPB's website or call the toll-free number to receive status updates, provide additional information, and review responses provided to the consumer by the company.

Throughout this process, Consumer Response is supported by CFPB colleagues who provide subject matter expertise and help monitor complaints involving certain groups.

# Results

## How Complaints Reach the CFPB

Between July 21 and December 31, 2011, the CFPB received 13,210 consumer complaints, including 9,307 credit card complaints and 2,326 mortgage complaints.[6,7]

Forty-four percent of all complaints were submitted through the CFPB's website and 14.7 percent via telephone calls. Referrals from other regulators accounted for 34.9 percent of all complaints received. The rest were submitted by mail, email, and fax.

The tables presented below show complaints by type, actions taken, company response, and consumer review of company responses.[8]

## Consumers' Credit Card Complaints

Table 1 shows the most common types of credit card complaints that the CFPB has received as reported by consumers. Over 69 percent of all credit card complaints fell into these 10 categories.

**Table 1. Most Common Credit Card Complaints Reported by Consumers**

| | # | % |
|---|---|---|
| Billing disputes | 1,278 | 13.7% |
| Identity theft / Fraud / Embezzlement | 1,014 | 10.9% |
| APR or interest rate | 950 | 10.2% |
| Other | 854 | 9.2% |
| Closing / Cancelling account | 478 | 5.1% |
| Credit reporting | 437 | 4.7% |
| Credit card payment / Debt protection | 383 | 4.1% |
| Collection practices | 378 | 4.1% |
| Late fee | 364 | 3.9% |
| Other fee | 334 | 3.6% |
| CREDIT CARD COMPLAINTS IN TOP 10 TYPES | 6,470 | 69.5% |

The CFPB has generally relied on the consumer's characterization of his or her complaint to identify the nature of it for analytical purposes, and the consumers are generally correct. However, the CPFB's experience to date suggests that consumers have different interpretations of what these categories mean. For example, one consumer might choose billing dispute to categorize a problem that another would describe as a concern with a provider's setting or changing of an interest rate. To improve the reliability of these data, the Bureau will clarify the consumer's options to promote more consistent categorization of complaints.

## Consumers' Mortgage Complaints

Table 2 shows the types of mortgage complaints that the CFPB has received as reported by consumers.

**Table 2. Types of Mortgage Complaints Reported by Consumers**

| | # | % |
|---|---|---|
| Applying for the loan (Application, originator, mortgage broker) | 235 | 10.1% |
| Receiving a credit offer (Credit decision/Underwriting) | 65 | 2.8% |
| Signing the agreement (Settlement process and costs) | 96 | 4.1% |
| Making payments (Loan servicing, payments, escrow accounts) | 501 | 21.5% |
| Problems when you are unable to pay (Loan modification, collection, foreclosure) | 889 | 38.2% |
| TOTAL MORTGAGE COMPLAINTS | 2,326 | 100.0% |

Nearly 60 percent of consumers filed complaints about making payments or problems when they are unable to pay. Consumers that have filed these complaints generally appear to be driven by a desire to seek agreement with their companies on foreclosure alternatives. As with credit card complaints, consumers appear to interpret these categories differently.

## How Companies Respond to Consumer Complaints

Approximately 9,885 (or 75 percent) of all complaints received between July 21 and December 31, 2011, were sent by Consumer Response to companies for review and response.[9] Table 3 shows how companies responded to these complaints during this time period.

Responses include a description of any steps taken or that will be taken in response to the complaint, communications received from the consumer as a result of any steps taken, any follow-up actions or planned follow-up actions in further response to the complaint, and categorization of the response. Beginning December 1, 2011, response category options included "closed with relief," "closed without relief," "in progress," and other administrative options. Relief is defined as objective, measurable, and verifiable monetary value to the consumer as a direct result of the steps taken or that will be taken in response to the complaint. Where a company responds "closed with relief," additional space is provided to describe that relief and to assign an estimated dollar amount.[10] "Closed without relief" indicates that the steps taken by the company in response to the complaint did not result in monetary value to the consumer that is objective, measurable, and verifiable, but may have addressed some or all of the consumer's complaint involving non-monetary requests. Consumers are given the option to review and dispute company responses with and without relief.

Companies responded to 88.1 percent of the complaints sent to them. Companies report closing over 55 percent of complaints with relief and approximately 31 percent without relief.

**Table 3. How Companies Have Responded to Consumer Complaints**

| | All | | Credit Card | | Mortgage | |
|---|---|---|---|---|---|---|
| | # | % | # | % | # | % |
| Company reported closed with relief | 5,476 | 55.4% | 4,785 | 64.1% | 306 | 18.6% |
| Company reported closed without relief | 3,028 | 30.6% | 2,069 | 27.7% | 768 | 46.7% |
| Company provided administrative response | 203 | 2.1% | 112 | 1.5% | 71 | 4.3% |
| Company reviewing | 1,178 | 11.9% | 497 | 6.7% | 498 | 30.3% |
| TOTAL COMPLAINTS SENT TO COMPANY | 9,885 | 100.0% | 7,463 | 100.0% | 1,643 | 100.0 % |

Beginning December 1, 2011, companies had the option to report an amount of relief with a response of "closed with relief." By December 31, 2011, companies had reported relief amounts in response to more than 500 complaints. The CFPB is reviewing reported relief amounts to ensure reporting is consistent with the CFPB's definition of relief.

## Consumers' Reviews of Companies' Responses

Once the company responds, the CFPB provides this response to the consumer for review. Where the company responds "closed with relief" or "closed without relief," consumers are given the option to dispute the response.[11] Complaints with disputed company responses are among those prioritized for investigation. Table 4 shows how consumers responded to the 7,349 complaints where they were given the option to dispute that companies report as closed or where full or partial resolution was reported. Consumers are asked to notify the CFPB within 30 days if they want to dispute a company's response. Nearly 40 percent of such consumers did not dispute the responses provided. Approximately 13 percent of consumers have disputed the responses provided. The rest were pending with consumers at the end of this period.

**Table 4. Consumer Review of Company Responses**

| | All | | Credit Card | | Mortgage | |
|---|---|---|---|---|---|---|
| | # | % | # | % | # | % |
| Pending consumer review of company's reported resolution | 3,488 | 47.5% | 2,400 | 41.3% | 809 | 77.4% |
| Consumer did not dispute company's reported resolution | 2,910 | 39.6% | 2,681 | 46.1% | 76 | 7.3% |
| Consumer disputed company's reported resolution | 951 | 12.9% | 734 | 12.6% | 160 | 15.3% |
| TOTAL COMPLAINTS FOR CONSUMER REVIEW | 7,349 | 100.0% | 5,815 | 100.0% | 1,045 | 100.0% |

## Consumer Response Investigations

After requesting that companies respond to all complaints filed and giving consumers the opportunity to review and dispute company responses, Consumer Response primarily focuses its review and investigation efforts on those complaints where the consumer disputed the response or where the company failed to provide a timely response. Consumer Response also periodically investigates groups of complaints to survey product- and issue-specific trends. Consumer Response investigations seek to determine why a company failed to provide a timely response (if applicable) and whether the consumer's dispute of the company's response (if applicable) justifies additional review with regard to the company's minimum required actions under the consumer financial protection laws within the CFPB's authority. In the course of an investigation, Consumer Response may ask companies and consumers for additional information. When a Consumer Response investigation is completed, Consumer Response sends the consumer a summary. In some cases, Consumer Response has referred complaints to colleagues in the CFPB's Division of Supervision, Enforcement, and Fair Lending and Equal Opportunity for further action.

Listening and responding to consumers is an integral part of the CFPB's work to understand issues in the financial marketplace. As Consumer Response processes complaints, it also continues to identify new ways to improve its processes to make them as efficient, effective, and easy-to-use as possible. The Bureau uses consumer complaints to inform its work in making prices and risks clearer, protecting consumers of financial products and services, and encouraging financial markets to operate fairly and competitively.

## End Notes

[1] Consumer complaints are submissions that express dissatisfaction with, or communicate suspicion of wrongful conduct by, an identifiable entity related to a consumer's personal experience with a financial product or service.

[2] Dodd-Frank Act, Public Law 111-203, Section 1021(c)(2).

[3] This report addresses the reporting requirement of Dodd-Frank, Public Law 111-203, Section 1013(b)(3)(c). Future reports will cover a preceding calendar year.

[4] If a particular complaint does not involve a product or market that is within the Bureau's jurisdiction or one currently being handled by the Bureau, Consumer Response refers it to the appropriate regulator.

[5] The CFPB initially requested that companies respond to complaints within 10 calendar days, but increased the requested response time to 15 calendar days when Consumer Response began handling mortgage complaints on December 1, 2011.

[6] This analysis excludes multiple complaints submitted by a given consumer on the same issue and whistleblower tips.

[7] All data are current as of December 31, 2011.

[8] Percentages in tables may not sum to 100 percent due to rounding.

[9] The remaining complaints have been referred to other regulatory agencies (10.9 percent), found to be incomplete (5.4 percent), or are pending with the consumer or the CFPB (4.7 percent and 4.2 percent, respectively).

[10] The CFPB initially asked companies to categorize their response as "full resolution provided," "partial resolution provided," "no resolution provided," or another administrative option. While companies' responses under the initial categorizations were maintained, for operational and reporting purposes responses categorized as "full resolution provided," or "partial resolution provided" are considered a subset of "closed with relief" and responses categorized as "no resolution provided" are considered a subset of "closed without relief."

[11] Initially consumers were given the option to dispute responses from companies that indicated a resolution had been provided. With the shift to closure categories, consumers are given the option to dispute both responses with and without relief.

# INDEX

## #



## A



## B

## C

## N



## O



## P

## Q



## R



## S

## T



## U



## V



## W



## Y